A *Survey of the* Black Church *in* America

Exploring Its History, Ministry, and Unique Strengths

TONY EVANS

MOODY PUBLISHERS

CHICAGO

This book is excerpted from *Oneness Embraced: A Kingdom Race Theology for Reconciliation, Unity, and Justice,* © 2011, 2022 by Anthony T. Evans (Moody Publishers).

Scripture quotations, unless otherwise indicated, are taken from the New American Standard Bible®, Copyright © 1960, 1962, 1963, 1968, 1971, 1972, 1973, 1975, 1977, 1995 by The Lockman Foundation. Used by permission. www. Lockman.org

Scripture quotations marked NIV are taken from the Holy Bible, New International Version®, NIV®. Copyright © 1973, 1978, 1984, 2011 by Biblica, Inc.™ Used by permission of Zondervan. All rights reserved worldwide. www.zondervan.com The "NIV" and "New International Version" are trademarks registered in the United States Patent and Trademark Office by Biblica, Inc.™

Edited by Kevin Mungons
Interior design: Ragont Design
Cover design: Erik M. Peterson
Cover photo: Public domain
Author photo: Tayte Gerik

Library of Congress Cataloging-in-Publication Data

Names: Evans, Tony, 1949- author.
Title: A survey of the Black church in America : exploring its history, ministry and unique strengths / by Tony Evans.
Description: Chicago, IL : Moody Publishers, [2023] | Includes bibliographical references and index. | Summary: "Evans opens our eyes to the black presence in the Scriptures and takes a focused look at the uniqueness and place of the black church. Evans faithfully interacts with movements such as Black Lives Matter, Critical Race Theory, and the 1619 Project. Evans provides a divine, clear, kingdom-focused perspective"-- Provided by publisher.
Identifiers: LCCN 2023031906 | ISBN 9780802425416 | ISBN 9780802476470 (ebook)
Subjects: LCSH: African American churches--History. | African Americans--Religion--History. | African American leadership--Religious aspects--Christianity. | Religion and culture--United States. | BISAC: RELIGION / Christian Church / History | RELIGION / Leadership
Classification: LCC BR563.N4 E9643 2023 | DDC 277.30089/96073—dc23/eng/20230814
LC record available at https://lccn.loc.gov/2023031906

Originally delivered by fleets of horse-drawn wagons, the affordable paperbacks from D. L. Moody's publishing house resourced the church and served everyday people. Now, after more than 125 years of publishing and ministry, Moody Publishers' mission remains the same— even if our delivery systems have changed a bit. For more information on other books (and resources) created from a biblical perspective, go to www.moodypublishers.com or write to:

Moody Publishers
820 N. LaSalle Boulevard
Chicago, IL 60610

1 3 5 7 9 10 8 6 4 2

Printed in the United States of America

A Survey of the
Black Church
in America

Contents

Chapter 1

The Importance of Understanding History

A s a teenager in 1968, I boarded a train and headed from Baltimore to Atlanta to attend Carver Bible College. Carver was a small black college that had been started by white fundamentalist missionaries to train "Negroes" in the Scriptures. I'll never forget arriving at Carver the very first time. I had expected a "college" to be large—I had expected something majestic. What greeted me was a few small rooms, a parking lot, some students, and a handful of professors. Carver wasn't my idea of college at all. But in those days, as a black American, I did not have many other better choices if I wanted to study the Bible.

Standing in that parking lot the very first day, I told myself I would only stay a year. Then I would move on and find something better that more resembled my idea of a college. But during that first year, I came to be mentored and taught by two men who took me under their wings and forever changed my life. One was a black man—Dr. John McNeal, the Dean of Students. Dr. McNeal quickly assumed the role of a father figure in my life. Recognizing my insatiable passion for learning and preaching the Word of God, he challenged me to always balance biblical study with personal spiritual depth. He also opened his home to me and encouraged me to spend as much time there as I wanted, with him and his wife, asking as many questions as I wanted about the Scriptures. Dr. McNeal knew the lack of strong biblical training in the black community at that time and he had made it his life mission to pour into the future of the black church in America by investing in her leaders while he could.

The other man who impacted my life was Dr. Howard Dial, a white professor who came to teach at Carver at the request of Dr. McNeal. They had worked together at another location where Dr. McNeal supervised Dr. Dial. At that time, Dr. Dial and his wife had their heart set on becoming missionaries overseas. But through their friendship and work relationship, Dr. McNeal explained the missional need for training black Christian men who would go on and pastor and lead churches in sound, biblical teaching. Dr. Dial accepted the calling to commit his life to investing in the lives of young men like me so that we could gain access to the biblical training that was mostly only available to white people at that time.

Due to the brilliance, compassion, love, and support of these two men, my one year at this small Bible college turned into four. I gave up my hopes of attending something bigger or grander. Instead, I realized the value of what I was receiving in my education there as well as the personal discipleship and mentoring I was able to maximize through a close personal relationship with both men.

Because Carver was located just minutes from the Atlanta University system that included Morris Brown, Morehouse, Clark, and Spellman colleges—the centerpieces of black educational and cultural life—there was never any lack of sociological discussion during my years there. Carver was also located just minutes from the Interdenominational Theological Center, which was a predominantly black seminary that emphasized black history, black culture, and black theology.

Here I was at a Bible college that stressed biblical theology, evangelism, and discipleship in the midst of a city of great diversity of thought of civil rights and black culture. You can imagine the confluence of perspectives that I was exposed to in an area so inundated with differing views. Students from ITC often challenged us from Carver about our relevance to the social realities that blacks were facing. Carver students challenged the students at ITC about their liberal orientation to Scripture. These debates, along with living in Atlanta in 1968 at the height of the civil rights movement, provoked questions in me that traditional theology had not clearly addressed. I began formulating answers to these questions out of a kingdom theology that continued to develop as I went deeper in my study of Scripture.

Living in Atlanta brought the issue of the black church, our racial history, and our role in society even more to the forefront of my mind because racism in Atlanta was more overt than it was in Baltimore where I had been raised. For example, one of my white "evangelical" professors asked me to do some work on his house for him one afternoon. When it came time for lunch, he put me in another room to eat by myself. He told me that his mother lived with him and that she would never eat with a black man. That was an eye-opening moment, one of many to come.

I also remember being very nervous when I had to drive through small Georgia towns because of the horror stories I had heard about the South. A white medical doctor had been told about my passion for theology and proclaiming God's Word at Carver, and had hired me to conduct an outreach Bible study to Christian blacks in his area. He paid my way and provided me with a place where I could sleep at night. As best as I can remember, though, he never once came to the Bible study he initiated.

The Bible study was located several hours away from Atlanta, making driving there an experience. The "n-word" got thrown at me if I was in an area where I needed to slow down. I saw black men and women walking with their heads held down. If I stopped for gas (I tried not to stop at all), I saw black men and women who wouldn't even make eye contact with the whites around them. These realities along with two major events affected me greatly toward devoting myself to theologically grappling with the contradiction between the white "evangelical" church and what it taught in comparison with the segregation that it was practicing. It stoked the fire in me to study, understand, and apply the strengths and uniqueness of the black church, which could benefit society at large.

One of these events was the time Lois and I visited Bob Jones University. Bob Jones University was a leading evangelical school that taught that the Bible was the inerrant Word of God, yet it also publicly practiced racial segregation. Not only did BJU publicly promote racial segregation, but it actively taught that it was biblical. Bob Jones Sr. preached and published a sermon titled "Is Segregation Scriptural?" in 1960, and a few years later, Bob Jones III said this in a magazine interview:

> A Negro is best when he serves at the table. . . . When he does that, he's doing what he knows how to do best. . . . And the Negroes who have ascended to positions in government, in education, this sort of thing, I think you'll find, by and large, have a strong strain of white blood in them.[1]

I will never forget driving onto the campus of this "Bible-based" university and being followed and stopped by the campus police not only to inquire what we were doing there, but to ask us to leave.

The second impacting event was when I attended Colonial Hills Baptist Church in East Point, Georgia, with my mentor and professor,

Howard Dial. As I mentioned earlier, Dr. Dial was white. He attended an all-white church. Yet he was also a committed Christian man who had a heart for racial reconciliation. He was the academic dean at Carver. Over my time there we became very good friends.

The Sunday I attended church as a guest of Dr. Dial just so happened to be the Sunday that the leading candidate for the vacant pastorate was preaching. He preached a powerful message while giving a call to come forward in a commitment to discipleship at the end. I responded to the call, not realizing that the focus would turn to me when I did.

First, the man who received me at the altar to pray with me made it clear, not only to me but to everyone in the church, that there was a monumental difference between making a spiritual commitment to discipleship and making a commitment to come to church. Those were two very separate deals.

Next, the leadership made it explicitly clear that they did not want blacks coming to the church on a regular basis. In fact, the church ended up splitting over this one event and the prospective pastor declined the invitation to become senior pastor, saying that he could not pastor a church steeped in racial segregation. Unaware to most at the time, a young Philip Yancey was sitting in the pews witnessing this whole situation take place as well. He would later go on to tell how this injustice within the body of Christ impacted the way he viewed spirituality and helped inform his role in seeking to bring clarity to it through his writing and ministry.[2]

These and other less dramatic events brought the major disconnection between evangelical belief and practice to light for me on a highly personal level. I understood afresh the anger and frustration of the black church in America at the hypocrisy of white Christianity in general and white evangelicalism in particular.

Experiencing firsthand the reality of what black theology and black power sought to correct propelled me to wrestle with theological issues at a deep level. I already had a passion that had been birthed in Baltimore and Philadelphia to address these issues, but studying in Atlanta at the height of the civil rights movement fired my passion to a supersonic level. In fact, it thrust me into a desire to study further at seminary so that I could address the issue not only from a popular level (such as a pulpit), but also from an academic level. I set my mind to bridge the divide both on theological and practical terms in a way that would be consistent with the kingdom concepts that I had been introduced to and had become extremely inquisitive about.

In August of 1972, Lois and I arrived at the campus of Dallas Theological Seminary. I was the fourth African American student ever accepted into the master's degree program at a school that had begun nearly fifty years earlier. The first three were Eddie Lane, Ruben Conner, and Ron Roberts.

Not wanting to distance myself from my own culture while learning in a nearly entirely white evangelical culture, I began attending a black church called Community Bible Church pastored by Dr. Ruben Conner. This provided me the contextual reality to keep before my theological queries.

The environment on the DTS campus was welcoming to me by most of the professors, but it also became clear that many of the students had not been around African Americans up until then. Therefore, either they didn't necessarily want to relate to us or just weren't quite sure how to do so. Some were reacting to the social climate and felt like the actions of the African American community were not keeping in line with how Christians should act. But what that meant to me was that, while not all of the actions they were witnessing on the news could be justified, the white students likewise did not understand the social, political, and economic realities that prompted much of what they were seeing and hearing about.

I would categorize the professors I had during that time into three distinct groups. The first group was very open and welcoming to me. They wanted to interact and initiated mutual engagement and discussions, inviting my perspective. Four who stand out to me the most were Howard Hendricks, Haddon Robinson, Charles Ryrie, and Gene Getz. All four, plus others, were very welcoming. I would often spend hours in their respective offices talking one on one. Or we would go to lunch together, or they would invite Lois and me to their homes for dinner.

The second group was clearly not comfortable. There would never be an outright rejection, but you could tell that they either didn't know how to interact with a black man or with the concerns of the culture, or simply resented having to do so. The third group was somewhat in the middle. They had chosen to go with the flow, as it were.

I'll never forget one of my earliest conversations with Dr. Walvoord, the president of Dallas Theological Seminary at the time. We were talking about the fact that Dallas Seminary had been segregated for so long. And while I realize he had addressed this issue as far back as the mid-1950s by saying the openness was there but that there were not any qualified African Americans to accept into the program, I felt that was an insufficient, and convenient, answer to the problem. Especially when no real effort had appeared to have taken place to locate qualified applicants. I wondered why, so I asked. His statement to me was, "Tony, I'm not a fighter. I kind of go with the law—the protocol." Another professor pastored a church in Dallas and informed me that the deacons at his church would not allow me to even visit. It was disconcerting to know that some of my professors still went to and pastored churches that practiced segregation. Perhaps the most influential church that was attended by many professors was First Baptist Church of Dallas, pastored by the late Dr. W. A. Criswell, who publicly proclaimed segregation based on the "curse of Ham," a position he recanted shortly before he died. That seemed to be the atmosphere of the Bible churches at that time. It was a culture of self-segregation without the overt rejection. It was subtle, but real.

This context is given as we begin our time together in this book to shed light on why I feel compelled to speak and write about the black church in America, and also to help the reader see the complexities that go into the history of the black church. The history of the black church is not a neat set of dates, locations, or names. Rather, it is a complex narrative speaking of a diaspora comprising a multiplicity of ethnicities from the continent of Africa somehow seeking a spiritual hub in an oppressed and limited environment.

When I finished my four-year ThM in 1976, having graduated with honors, I decided to look for another school to pursue my doctoral degree. That was when I called James Cone, the founder of black theology. I wanted to find out more about the program he taught because I had been challenged from reading his material, even though we used a different hermeneutic to address issues. Dr. Cone had captivated me with his insistence that God's perspective on this issue of racial disparity and oppression was not a minor biblical theme.

I enjoyed our phone conversation. He was a very warm and friendly man, but due to other reasons, I eventually decided to pursue my doctorate at DTS. However, I chose to make Dr. Cone's theology the topic for my doctoral research and dissertation. During this time, I was also invited to become an associate professor. Simultaneously, Dr. Ruben Conner and Dr. Gene Getz challenged me to start a Bible church in Dallas under Black Evangelistic Enterprises as a way of modeling the ideas that I had percolating within me resulting from my theological training and burden for connecting the spiritual and social state of my community. These ideas had become foundational concepts for what would become a kingdom perspective on ministry.

Lois and I prayed about whether I should be a full-time professor at the seminary or whether I should start a church. Being a professor would have been a lot easier for me at that time with a wife and small children and a doctoral program to complete. However, Dr. Getz encouraged me instead to live out my beliefs. He and his church also committed to financially support this effort over the initial years of starting up a church. Dr. Getz had a calling and desire to see the black church in America strengthened, and he worked, often behind the scenes, in significant efforts to strengthen and spread the black church's footprint.

So, after being confirmed by God that this is what He wanted us to do, interestingly enough over a dinner at Dr. Ryrie's home, Lois and I agreed to begin a church in the southern section of Dallas. That is when I also became an adjunct professor at DTS.

Oak Cliff Bible Fellowship was organized on June 6, 1976, in our home with about ten people who joined us for a weekly Bible study. We set forth a vision of building a church that would not only be about making disciples, but would also have a social impact in the community. As the church began to grow, these concepts of connecting the spiritual and the social began to be implemented through ministries designed to affect our community. I aimed to establish a church that would reflect the heartbeat of my culture and meet the needs of my community while integrating a higher study of and understanding of scriptural principles and truths. Over four decades later, our church has grown even larger than I ever hoped and has been used by God through His grace to impact people locally and—through our national ministry, The Urban Alternative—even worldwide.

In looking back on how God shaped my perspective and opened doors for me through so many caring and well-positioned individuals, I know that I have been blessed. I am aware that not everyone has this path and that for many, if not most, black Americans, it is an even more uphill climb than I experienced. This is largely due to the devastating impacts racism, inequality, and even the hotbed phrase "systemic racism" has produced.

When you understand that in a sprint some racers are allowed to get started quicker or are allowed to start at a point much farther ahead of another group—and the rest of the group spends their whole time just trying to catch up because the sprint is intrinsically inequitable—it may help in the level of empathy you have about this historical reality of the separate worlds many blacks and whites live in. When you can grasp this reality, and how frequently it appears in our culture—especially its resultant cyclical effects—it can give you a different sensitivity to the conversations at hand or historical realities of institutions such as churches. And while the existence of racism cannot and must not be used as a reason for not accepting and maximizing personal and corporate responsibility, neither should we ignore its realities and impacts over time. In studying the history of the black church in America, it is a large part of the story.

The root of the racial problems we face in our nation today are clearly spiritual. It's only when we identify and understand the spiritual components that we are then able to translate them to the pragmatic realities of the cultural crisis at hand.

As an African American, my vision was formed in the pragmatic reality of racial disparity that caused me to focus on questions about race, oneness, and justice in church history that many of my white counterparts did not have to address. This dualism forced me to read Scripture to shed light on these issues. I had to look not only to the theology but also the practical application of that theology within the *Sitz im Laben*—or situation in life—for how that theology fleshes out.

White evangelicalism often expressed belief in the right things concerning the oneness of the body of Christ, but throughout history it did not consistently apply this belief system in either the church or the culture. In fact, the white church became a primary means, through either or both explicit and complicit manners, of justifying the racism and injustices perpetuated within the broader culture. Its overt racism and segregation—as well as its silence about injustice, human dignity, and racism—allowed it to become a co-conspirator to the generational perpetuation of racist views and actions throughout all the structures and systems of society. These include the family, educational institutions, law, government, business, and economic development. While there have always been individuals and groups in white culture who wanted to apply the right practice of this belief—remnants such as the Quakers, the abolitionists, and the white freedom marchers, among others whom I have mentioned by name and who have helped me personally—they did not always have a paradigm through which to express it, nor do they always have that today. There has existed a dichotomy, making it difficult to implement the applicational truth of not only oneness, but also biblical justice. As Dr. Warren Wiersbe, renowned white Bible teacher and father to many in the ministry, acknowledged, this roadblock often led to an ignoring of these and like issues in the white church. He wrote,

> We are handicapped in the white church. If I preached Jesus' first sermon (Luke 4:14–30) and gave it the social emphasis that He gave, our church has no vehicle for doing anything about the problem. People would respond in one of two ways: 1) "This preacher is off base, so let's get rid of him," or 2) "I've never seen it quite that way, but what do I do next?" For the most part, our white churches don't have the instruments, the organizational structure, to get involved in social action. Our usual solution is to put some inner-city organization into the budget or maybe to collect and distribute used clothing. . . . When it comes to racial issues, many white churches will participate in any number of symbolic activities, but they're hesitant when you ask them to get involved in sacrificial services in the trenches.[3]

Promise Keepers, the men's movement that became popular in the 1980s and 1990s and at which I spoke on numerous occasions, experienced this as a parachurch movement. Churches were happy to send their men to listen to a black preacher, or hug a minority person in attendance and verbally commit to racial reconciliation (Promise 6 out of 7). But when it came to diving deeper into the sin of racism, what might be done to address it, the repentance needed for it, and the actions that follow repentance, many churches pulled back. "Mark Pollard, a special associate of Promise Keepers in the 1990s, remembers that major donors started to back away, saying they weren't interested if Promise Keepers was going to be a civil rights organization. As he traveled the country with Promise Keepers founder Coach Bill McCartney planning and promoting events, Pollard, who is Black, was also asked again and again why race should be an issue at all. Wasn't the gospel colorblind?"[4] Not long after this greater push for reconciliation, the funding for PK began to dry up.

Yet although difficulties and challenges exist, their presence should never be the criteria for whether we give up or keep trying. Views of theology formulated through the lens of any culture will not only produce a myopic view, but also the resultant effects of an inability to carry out the true teaching in Scripture. This inability not only affects those who would be the recipients of the ministry outreaches, but it also affects those doing the ministry because it limits God's involvement in what is being done. Only when biblical truth is the absolute standard by which thoughts and actions are aligned will we experience the full manifestation of God's glory, purposes, and plans in the body of Christ. Maintaining an informational and otherworldly view of theology while neglecting a holistic view of God's kingdom aborts any real opportunity for application. That's why studying the true stories of history and what has shaped our churches as we know them today is important. God desires that we live and work together in order to advance His kingdom agenda on earth. But living and working together becomes difficult if we do not truly know each other and each other's authentic histories.

One of the elements of God's kingdom agenda is His heart for oneness, also known as unity. Unity can be defined in its simplest of terms as oneness of purpose. It is working together in harmony toward a shared vision and goal.

Unity is not uniformity, nor is it sameness. Just as the Godhead is made up of three distinct coequal persons (i.e., the Trinity)—the Father, the Son, and the Holy Spirit—each unique in personhood and yet at the same time one in essence, unity reflects a oneness that does not negate individuality. Unity does not mean everyone needs to be like everyone else. God's creative variety is replete with displaying itself through a humanity crafted in different shapes, colors, and styles. Each of us, in one form or another, is unique. Unity occurs when we combine our unique differences together as we head toward a common goal. It is the sense that the thing that we are gathered for and moving toward is bigger than our own individual preferences.

Through the establishment of the church, along with His overarching rulership above it, God has created a reflection of His kingdom in heaven on earth. He has reconciled racially divided groups into one new man (Eph. 2:14–15), uniting them into a new body (Eph. 2:16), so that the church can function in unity (Eph. 4:13). The church is the place where racial, gender, and class distinctions are no longer to be divisive because of our unity and identity in Christ (Gal. 3:28). This does not negate differences that remain intact—*oneness* simply means that those differences are embraced. Joining our unique strengths together, we add strength to strength, making a more complete and balanced whole based on our mutual relationship with and commitment to Christ. Biblical unity does not create color-blindness, but rather gives divine purpose to the diversity of color-uniqueness.

The issue of oneness in the church is so important that we are told to look out for people who seek to undermine it (Rom. 16:17). In fact, God promised to judge those who divide His church (1 Cor. 3:17).

This is because the church is to reflect the values of the kingdom of God to a world in desperate need of experiencing Him.

The church is the only authentic cross-racial, cross-cultural, and cross-generational basis for oneness in existence. It is the only institution on earth obligated to live under God's authority while enabled to do so through His Spirit. In 1 Corinthians 12:12–13, Paul wrote:

> For even as the body is *one* and yet has many members, and all the members of the body, though they are many, are *one* body, so also is Christ. For by *one* Spirit we were all baptized into *one* body, whether Jews or Greeks, whether slaves or free, and we were all made to drink of *one* Spirit (italics added).

The baptism of the Spirit at the moment of salvation, the act whereby God places us into the body of Christ, secures the oneness God wants us to have. This inimitable work of the Spirit positions us under the rule of God. The Greek word for baptism used in the Bible means identification. It was used when a cloth maker dipped cloth into dye so that the cloth would take on the color of the dye. The cloth was then said to be baptized, or identified, with the dye.

When we got saved, we were baptized into the body of Christ. We are now identified with a new family, having been placed into a new spiritual environment while still on earth. No matter what our race, gender, or class, when we came to Jesus Christ we entered into God's oneness because we came under His authority.

That is why Ephesians 4:3 says that we are to "preserve the unity of the Spirit." The Scripture uses the term *preserve*, indicating that we don't create unity. Authentic unity, then, cannot be mandated or manufactured. This is so because God desires that His standards alone serve as the basis, criteria, and foundation for oneness. It is also why He thwarts attempts at unity and globalization that ignore or exclude Him (Gen. 11:1–9). The Spirit created unity when we were saved. Our job is to find out what the Spirit has already done so that we can live, walk in, and embrace that reality in the black church, white church, or multi-ethnic churches in our land. In this way, we will gain greater ground in expanding God's glory and advancing His kingdom agenda on earth.

Chapter 2

The Myth of Inferiority

S ecular history has often excluded the whole truth from its record of accounts. It has rewritten the annals of our foundation to offer a one-sided and limited view of many things. An important area it has distorted, for the purposes of this book, is the founding of our nation. Even though African Americans were involved and present, as freed men and not only as slaves, in the critical junctures of the birthing of our land, our history books, mainstream movies, and often even our artistic renditions show little or no racial diversity. African American heroes of such important battles such as the Battle of Bunker Hill are not only completely absent from mainstream historical accounts, but also, more recently, explained away out of paintings made by those who witnessed the battle firsthand.

What this has done in the American psyche is elevate one group of people, white Americans, above all others. Not only does it disconnect African Americans from any personal heritage to our nation, but it also offers an incomplete and inaccurate view of ourselves. An erroneous view of oneself, or a misguided view of another, as is the case when whites are taught an anemic view of black achievement and involvement in our land and churches, leads to actions that perpetuate the illusion, on both sides.

Just over a year before the Liberty Bell rang out calling all to come hear the Declaration of Independence, a young Paul Revere took his well-known Midnight Ride. Few of us who have been raised under the tutelage of our country are unaware of this ride. Yet how many of us know that on the very same night, a black man, Wentworth Cheswell, the freed grandson of a slave, also rode a Midnight Ride?[3] Cheswell was the first black judge, elected in 1768, a devoted husband, church member, and father of thirteen children. For forty-nine years, he served our nation in some form of public office such as auditor, assessor, moderator, and "town father."

Cheswell's commission as messenger, given to him by the Committee of Safety, was the same as that given to Revere. Wentworth Cheswell rode north. Paul Revere rode west. Both had a part to play in the fight for the American Revolution. Cheswell's alerting those in the north to make haste and organize themselves to head south for the imminent conflict with the British served our country just as well. Yet Wentworth Cheswell is virtually nowhere to be found in our historical accounts.

Likewise, as the Liberty Bell cracked, creating a gap on the day honoring George Washington, another gap exists in the retelling of the historic accomplishments of the general. This gap belongs to a man named James Armistead. The ending of the American Revolution with the victory at Yorktown and the capture of British general Charles Cornwallis, from a historical perspective, is attributed to General Washington and his troops.

Yet what has been often left out of the retelling of this event is that Washington was able to do what he did with as minimal loss in soldiers' lives that he had—less than a minuscule 1 percent casualty rate—due to information supplied to him that had been acquired by James Armistead, a black man. Posing as a runaway slave and

British spy, Armistead gathered important intelligence for General Washington (see the account later in this chapter).

Similarly, the contributions of the black church have often been neglected or marginalized, thus hindering the oneness of the collective American church. This lack of truth in our education has fed what is known as the "myth of inferiority" within the black culture. It has also fed the "myth of superiority" in the white culture.

When a person is told either directly or subliminally that the definition of "good," "pretty," or "smart" comes clothed in a certain color, or that he is a "boy," even if he is the senior to the one making the designation, the psychological damage can be overpowering. Or consider what happens when black children are told they are "at risk" simply because of their skin color. Doesn't this decrease their motivation to learn and validate some teachers' belief that black children are unable to learn?[1] The myth of inferiority hits its mark time and time again.

When I was in junior high school, for example, many of my Anglo teachers had limited expectations for my future, and thus they limited their challenges to me. Rarely did they speak to my African American classmates and me about becoming doctors, lawyers, or the president of the United States. This implied that those positions were either reserved for whites or available for only a few blacks who could only serve other blacks, whereas, of course, white professionals could serve both the black and white communities. It would take a Jewish man, Martin Resnick, whom I worked for, as well as a black man, B. Sam Hart, whom I served under in his ministry, to encourage me to even consider attending college. College wasn't on my radar until these men brought it up. College wasn't something our teachers or schools even hinted at for most blacks in that day.

From the days of slavery until the present, the inferiority myth has been passed down through the generations, leaving its devastating psychological thumbprint. It is a subtle form of psychological oppression, but it leaves its ugly stains wherever it goes. A contemporary manifestation of the myth's impact is visibly demonstrated in the overly dependent posture of the black community on government-based social service programs.

The independent black church during slavery countered the inferiority myth, and instead hewed out a community, culture, religious institution, and antislavery movement with limited support from the government or broader culture. This is indicative of a strong church foundation comprised of highly functioning and independent individuals. It led the way in exposing and addressing the false narrative of the myth. Unfortunately, though, the heightened infiltration of the inferiority myth into the black psyche, an unforeseen negative by-product of integration, is seen in the black community's inability to rise above an often self-imposed plethora of destructive characteristics grounded in a victim mentality. In this vein there has developed an illegitimate and unbiblical dependence on government to do what should squarely rest in the scope of the family and the church.

One might argue that the present realities of a large segment of the black community are not a result of the existence of the inferiority myth, but rather a result of systemic racist structures in the broader society or cultural weaknesses within the black community. However, when the actions of those who illegitimately feign superiority dictate the negative actions of others over extended generations, then others must, of necessity, feel inferior to some degree in order to succumb to such dictation.

This illegitimate superiority has been reinforced not only through our legal system, language, family structure, and educational system but through our churches as well. The resultant psychological effects of the myth on African Americans have been devastating, culminating by and large in contemporary society through a culture punctuated by definitions of defeatism and victimization.

What's worse is that our own education system, for both black and white, perpetuated the myth. This further engrained into the minds of our nation's citizens, producing an unnatural division. I'm positioning this content toward the start of this book on the history of the black church because examining this aspect of our culture reveals the context in which this history was lived out and took place.

One reason this myth became so embedded into each of us is because one of the first things kids were taught about our history in school is that blacks were descendants of slaves who arrived in America from the west coast of Africa. In contrast, kids were taught that whites were the creators of Western civilization—in Greece, Rome, France, England, America—thereby producing the first physician of antiquity, Hippocrates; the father of history, Herodotus; great philosophers, Socrates and Plato; and the great scientists, Galileo and Sir Isaac Newton.

Rarely were our children taught about the great nations of north, east, and central Africa, and if they were, they were never taught that all of Africa, including Egypt and Ethiopia, was initially occupied and dominated by blacks. Academia never broadcasted the name Imhotep—a distinguished physician in Egyptian history who practiced medicine before Greece became a nation. Academia never recognized Manatheo—who wrote the history of Egypt before Herodotus was born. Nor was anyone taught about Queen Ti—who once ruled Egypt and whose statues leave no doubt that she was black.

White children left history classes knowing countries and names of white heroes and heroines. On the other hand, black children left history classes without educators or textbooks acknowledging the accomplishments by those from or in Africa at all, which include producing clocks and calendars, maps, gears, great architecture, engineering, medicine, and mathematics. For example, Africans were the first ones who named and mapped the stars and were the first to teach students from Greece on African soil, and much more. A sampling of the heroes of African descent, often neglected from Western education, include:

Benjamin Banniker

Benjamin Banniker was a mathematician, astronomer, compiler of almanacs, inventor, and writer. Banniker was a freeman in the slave state of Maryland and was raised on a farm near Baltimore. He was largely self-educated from books that he would borrow and read.

Around twenty years old, Banniker built a wooden clock that kept precise time. It is noted to be the first clock wholly made in the United States (and kept perfect time even until after his death in 1806). Shortly after, he was encouraged to study astronomy, which he also excelled in. By 1788, he began making astronomical calculations, and he accurately predicted a solar eclipse that occurred in 1789. From there, he began making other astronomical observations, including predicting other solar eclipses ten years ahead of time.

Banniker's most significant accomplishment was working on the surveying team and designing the layout for Washington, DC, and engaging with some of the country's founders in a way no black man had before. Furthermore, as a freeman, he opposed slavery and advocated civil rights—continually sending letters to US leaders, asking for aid in bringing about better conditions for African Americans.

Joseph Bologne

Joseph Bologne was born in Guadeloupe to a prominent French plantation owner and an African slave but moved to France as a teenager.

Because of his elite skill in fencing and horsemanship, he was assigned as an officer of the king's bodyguard and acquired the title Chevalier de Saint-Georges. This was a man of extraordinary talent. He was a champion fencer, master violinist and harpsichordist, classical music composer, and even became a colonel in the French Revolution.

By 1771, he became the concertmaster and music director of a leading symphony in Paris. In 1775, the Paris Opera was considering his nomination to be the next director. However, three of its leading women opposed him because he was a "mulatto." To avoid embarrassing the queen, Bologne withdrew his name. Nevertheless, he continued to write and direct esteemed operas and classical compositions.

Unfortunately, people called him "The Black Mozart." It may seem like a compliment, but in reality, it was and is demeaning. Bologne doesn't need to be compared to anybody, but rather celebrated for who he was and what he did. He was the first classical composer of African ancestry, and President John Adams called him "the most accomplished man in Europe."

James Armistead

James Armistead, an enslaved African American spy during the American Revolution, was born into slavery in Virginia around 1748. In 1781, he volunteered to join the US Army and enlisted in the Revolutionary War.

He served under Marquis de Lafayette, the commander of allied French forces. Armistead was employed as a spy. At great personal risk, Armistead posed as a runaway slave and pretended to be a British spy, all the while gaining the confidence of General Benedict Arnold and General Charles Cornwallis. The officers spoke freely in front of Armistead concerning their strategies. Armistead's reports documented the movements of the British, giving General Washington all that he needed to bring about a swift end to the war, saving innumerable American lives.

The ending of the American Revolution with the victory at Yorktown and the capture of General Cornwallis, from a historical perspective, is attributed to General Washington and his troops. However, this was only made possible because of the information gained by James Armistead, and we should celebrate him for his patriotic actions.

Richard Allen

Richard Allen, who was born into slavery, originally had no last name—he was simply known as "Negro Richard." At age seventeen, he converted and began preaching at the local Methodist churches in Delaware and on his plantation. In 1783, he was allowed to purchase his freedom, and he gave himself the last name Allen.

As a free man, Allen settled in Philadelphia and attended St. George's Methodist Church. His preaching and leadership attracted many blacks to the church and caused racial tension. You see, though blacks and whites worshiped together, there was still no equality. Worship was segregated, and blacks were treated poorly. Due to this, Allen left St. George's in 1787 and organized an independent Methodist church. However, Methodist leaders in Philadelphia continued to harass him. Finally, in 1816, Allen formally separated from the Methodist church and established a new denomination, the African Methodist Episcopal Church (AME). He focused on organizing a denomination in which free black people could worship without racial oppression and enslaved people could find a measure of dignity.

Today, AME has over six thousand churches and over two million members.

Mary Seacole

Mary Seacole's mother was Jamaican, and her father was a Scottish lieutenant in the British Army. Being multiracial (legally classified as a "mulatto" woman), she could not vote, hold public office, or enter the workforce.

However, Mary acquired nursing skills from her mother who

ran a boarding house for sick soldiers. To increase her knowledge and medical expertise, she traveled all over the Caribbean, Central America, and England. In 1854, she returned to England during the height of the Crimean War with a heart to serve. However, the British War Office turned her away. Undeterred, she created the "British Hotel," which was nursing quarters positioned behind the battle lines. She nursed wounded soldiers back to good health. She even traveled to the battlefield seeking out injured soldiers to help. Not only did she save numerous lives, but she also became well known among all the soldiers who affectionately called her "Mother Seacole."

In 2004, Mary was voted number one in the 100 Great Black Britons poll. Today, she is celebrated as a pioneering nurse who overcame the tremendous prejudice of being a biracial woman.

Henry Ossawa Tanner

Henry Ossawa Tanner was an African American painter born in Pennsylvania. His father was a minister and tried to discourage Henry's interest in art, but to no avail. However, his father's faith did influence him, as most of his paintings carried biblical themes.

At twenty-one, Tanner enrolled in the prestigious Pennsylvania Academy of the Fine Arts as the only African American student. In 1891, he traveled to Paris and enrolled at the Académie Julian. During his time abroad, his paintings brought him notoriety. In 1893, he traveled back to Pennsylvania, where he was met and spurned by racial prejudice. Therefore, he left the United States and returned to Paris.

By 1894, his paintings were exhibited at the annual Paris Salon. Over the years, he won awards for *Daniel in the Lions' Den* and *The Raising of Lazarus*—a rare accomplishment for an American artist and even more uncommon for an African American. Tanner's paintings continued to win awards in Paris and finally in America as well.

In 1969, long after his death, the Smithsonian honored him

through the first major solo exhibition of a black artist in the United States, recognizing Tanner as the first African American painter to gain international acclaim.

Charlotta Bass

Charlotta Bass was a remarkable woman who has, unfortunately, largely been forgotten like so many others. In 1952, she became the first black woman to run for vice president in the United States.

Bass received endorsements from prominent civil rights leaders like Paul Robeson and W. E. B. DuBois. Though her ticket virtually stood no chance of winning, as the Voting Rights Act did not exist and schools were still segregated, it still gave her a platform to raise awareness on racial issues.

Voicing concerns over the treatment of African Americans wasn't new to Bass. She was a longtime editor, publisher, and eventually owner of *The California Eagle*, the West Coast's oldest and most circulated black newspaper. For forty years, she used the newspaper to shed light on racial issues, including police brutality, discriminatory hiring and housing practices, and glorification of the Ku Klux Klan.

She denounced both political parties for neglecting black and women's rights, and she took an uncompromising stance against racial injustices. Both actions resulted in numerous death threats. She was labeled a communist and placed under FBI and CIA surveillance. Though she was viewed as being radical, she accomplished her main goal: placing racial equality in the national spotlight.

Bessie Coleman

Bessie Coleman was raised in Waxahachie, Texas, not far from where I live. She excelled in school and had a proclivity for mathematics. Therefore, Coleman avoided working in the cotton fields.

At twenty-three, she moved to Chicago and made her living as a beautician. She became interested in the field of aviation and dreamed of flying. However, discrimination prevented her from entering aviation school. She did not stop her pursuit. Instead, she learned French and, in 1920, was accepted at the Caudron Brothers School of Aviation in Le Crotoy, France.

On June 15, 1921, she became the first black person to gain an international pilot's license, and the first black woman and Native American to hold a pilot's license. Coleman returned to the United States, where the double stigma of racial and gender biases prevented her becoming a commercial pilot. Therefore, she specialized in stunt flying and parachuting because those were her only career options.

In 2007, the city of Waxahachie unveiled the Bessie Coleman official Texas historical marker at Freedman Memorial Plaza, and Mayor David Hill declared January 26 as Bessie Coleman Day in the city of Waxahachie.

Sandy Frederick Ray

Sandy Frederick Ray was a close friend of Martin Luther King Sr. Martin's son, King Jr., viewed Ray as a father figure and called him "Uncle Sandy."

Ray served Baptist churches in Georgia, Illinois, and Ohio, where he became an acclaimed Sunday radio preacher and the first black representative elected to the Ohio State Legislature. In 1944, Ray felt called to Cornerstone Baptist Church in Brooklyn, New York, where he pastored until his death. In ten years, under Ray's leadership, Cornerstone grew from 2,500 to 5,500 members, added multiple buildings and a daycare, and established a credit union.

People traveled to Brooklyn to hear Ray's dynamic preaching, but he also used his voice and platform to advance civil rights. In July 1957, Ray invited Billy Graham to preach on the steps outside his church. More than three thousand people attended to hear Graham preach against racist segregationist laws, calling for changes to legislation at the national level. Ray remained close to the King family. He fundraised for and assisted King Jr. during his arrests, supported the Montgomery bus boycotts, publicly rebuked southern white supremacists, and condemned segregation before the House Committee. King Jr. said that Ray was one of the strongest orators in the African American church. He should be celebrated for his faithfulness in ministry and involvement in civil rights.

Vivien Thomas

Vivien Thomas, the grandson of a slave, became a heart surgery pioneer. In 1930, Thomas became a laboratory assistant for Dr. Alfred Blalock at Vanderbilt University. However, because of institutional racism, he was classified and paid as a janitor. Nevertheless, Thomas rapidly mastered complex surgical techniques and research methodology.

In 1941, Blalock became Chief of Surgery at Johns Hopkins and Thomas accompanied him. It was there that Thomas and Blalock created a solution for "blue baby syndrome." In the 1940s, operating on the heart was unthinkable. However, Thomas created a blue baby–like condition in a dog, then corrected the condition through heart surgery. Over two years, he successfully performed the procedure on over two hundred dogs.

In 1944, the first procedure on a human baby was successful. Thomas coached Blalock throughout the operation from a stepstool. However, Thomas received no credit from Blalock or the medical field.

It took more than twenty-five years before Thomas received public recognition for his role in creating the blue baby surgery. In 1976, Johns Hopkins University awarded him an honorary doctorate and established the Vivien Thomas Fund to increase diversity at Johns Hopkins University School of Medicine, thus honoring his memory by removing for others the economic and racial barriers that often stood in his way.

Mahalia Jackson

Mahalia Jackson was born on October 26, 1911, in New Orleans, Louisiana. She was known as "the Queen of Gospel" and honored as one of the greatest musical figures in US history.

Jackson began singing when she was four years old at Mount Moriah Baptist Church. She moved to Chicago at sixteen and joined the Greater Salem Baptist Church. She sang with the Johnson Gospel Singers for a few years before working on solo projects with the gospel composer Thomas A. Dorsey.

Jackson was raised in a devout Christian home, but her style was influenced by the blues. In 1947, her song "Move On Up a Little Higher" sold millions of copies and became the highest selling gospel single in history. From there, Jackson successfully toured nationally and internationally, and even had her own gospel program on television.

Jackson was also active in the civil rights movement. She sang at the inauguration of President John F. Kennedy in 1961, the March on Washington, DC, in 1963 (right before the "I Have a Dream" speech), and at the funeral of Dr. Martin Luther King Jr. in 1968.

George Liele

George Liele, a freed Georgia slave, was one of the most significant figures in the history of Christian missions. He was the first American missionary, and the first Baptist missionary to take the gospel abroad.

Liele became a Christian in 1773 when he was twenty-three. Shortly after, he gained his freedom and began preaching for two years in slave quarters around Georgia and South Carolina. In 1775, Liele became the first ordained African American Baptist preacher in America, and he planted First African Baptist Church in 1777, a church that still gathers today.

However, racial persecution caused Liele to flee to Jamaica in

1782. But once there, Liele used this situation as an opportunity to plant a church, preach the gospel to Jamaican slaves, and begin public baptisms. His evangelism brought more persecution, and he was thrown in prison for "agitating slaves." Eventually, he was acquitted. Nevertheless, he continued to preach, baptize, and build the church.

By 1814, his missionary efforts helped produce eight thousand Jamaican Baptists, and that number grew to over twenty thousand by 1832. Liele's ministry had a significant spiritual impact on Jamaica, but it also made a social difference as well. By July 31, 1838, slavery was eradicated in Jamaica. Both these feats are a testimony to his legacy, and we should celebrate Liele for his lifelong missionary work.

There are so many more, such as Frederick Douglass, the runaway slave who subsequently published his autobiography, founded and ran the *North Star* newspaper, and was heralded by President Abraham Lincoln as a statesman, an orator, and a key voice for freedom and equality not only for blacks but also for women's rights. Also, Dr. Percy Lavon Julian—a scientist who synthesized sterol from the oil of a soybean to create synthetic hydrocortisone, reducing the cost of purchase for the general public from hundreds of dollars to mere cents—was the first to mass-produce physostigmine, a treatment for glaucoma, and paved the way for the invention of the birth control pill. And Matthew Alexander Henson, an able seaman from his early teen years, was the first man to place his foot on the North Pole.

Myths breed and grow in an atmosphere of ignorance. When we fail to teach the truth about our history and the many leading contributions those of African descent have made, the myth is left to leave its mark on the collective psyche of mankind. Myths often have a replicating effect when allowed to remain, by all parties involved.

Sacralization is the divergence from a comprehensive theology and a biblical worldview into the development of religious beliefs intended to serve the interest of a particular ethnic or racial group.

Supported by tradition or generalized prejudices, it is often formulated to carry out a specific end result or to justify a specific behavior.

Sacralization often leads to the creation or furtherance of damaging and devastating myths. One myth that helps us comprehend the historicity of the black experience and black evangelicalism implicitly and explicitly is this inferiority myth of black people to white people.

I will never forget the constant word pictures painted for me as a child that were designed to instill the inferiority myth within me. There were the White Tower restaurants that made it unmistakably clear that "colored people" were not good enough to eat there. I remember the "whites only" signs at places of business and the signs that pointed to inferior rear entrances and read "colored people enter here."

Then there were the white churches that praised God on Sunday as we did but would not allow my family to worship there. My father would say, "Son, they believe that God meant for the races to be kept separate, even when it comes to worshiping Him."

I knew the inferiority myth had taken root when as a budding adolescent I thought, along with many of my contemporaries, *Maybe it would be better if I had been born white.* This was the beginning of my love/hate relationship with seeing myself. Loving the personality God had given me, while questioning the package it was wrapped in.

Myths are traditions passed down over time in story form as a means of explaining or justifying events that are lacking in either scientific evidence or historical basis. The study of myths and mythology gives great insights into how societies answer questions about the nature of the world and the role of people in it. One very important element of myths is their ability to explain social systems, customs, and ways of life. Myths explain, to some degree, why people act the way they do.

Myths often have strong religious tenets associated with them. Whereas folktales and legends are developed and told for entertainment and amusement, myths are viewed as sacred and, therefore, true. For example, Greek mythology explained good and evil through the creation of stories, such as "Pandora's Box," and through the development of its pantheon of gods.

Myths are powerful because they are believed and therefore become the basis of our actions as individuals, as families, and as a society at large. Myths develop like a pearl inside an oyster's shell. When a grain of sand gets caught in the oyster's shell, it is continuously coated by the secretions of the oyster until a valuable pearl is formed. In the same way, the continuous secretions of societal standards, justified by religious principles, create a mythical pearl that is accepted as both valid and valuable by society.

These myths are accepted by a majority of people and their leaders, and as a result, they become embedded in the culture and through family training. Formal education, politics, religion, economics, science, and every other arena of life are defined by the myth and its traditions. Furthermore, myths tend to authenticate themselves and become self-fulfilled prophecy. Once this happens, nothing short of a catastrophic upheaval can change or reverse them. This is why Jesus had such a difficult time with the Pharisees of His day; their traditions had become so embedded in the fiber of Jewish life that the people wouldn't understand and accept the truth. Fighting myths can often label you as a "revolutionary."

When myths settle in and become traditions, they are then institutionalized, and the culture can hardly define itself without an intrinsic appeal to the myths that help create it and serve to maintain it. Education, politics, religion, economics, science, and every other arena of life are fair game for the myths' influence. Since myths tend to pervade all of society, there is no easy way to get away from them. Furthermore, myths tend to authenticate themselves; after all, everybody believes or accepts them, and this false belief system becomes a predictor of future behavior.

Acceptance of the myth that African Americans are inferior to

Anglos has had catastrophic consequences for the psyche of black people, the worldview of white people, and harmony among the races. Worst of all, it has hindered the church from being salt and light in America.

On one hand, this myth has kept the white church from appreciating the black church's great contributions to a true understanding of biblical Christianity and from incorporating those contributions into its own church life and doctrine. You can't appreciate what you do not know. On the other hand, the myth has kept the black community from fully embracing our own heritage and using it as a foundation for addressing the cataclysmic crisis of the African American community.

Spiritual assessments carry great weight in a culture's ability to understand itself as a whole as well as its components. When a culture allows a myth to dominate the way various groups within that culture relate to each other and to themselves, there will be disharmony, injustice, and inequity on every level of that culture. Such has been and still is the case in America. This reality has led to our society's inability to understand itself—and what we do not understand, we cannot fix.

The Creation of the Myth

The American myth of the inferior nature of African people began when the European slave traders subjugated Africans and exported them to the New World without having any understanding of this previously unknown people.

Dr. William Banks, author of *The Black Church in the United States*, describes how traders rationalized their actions through religious purposes:

> The Portuguese and Spanish were the first Europeans to deal in the black slave trade. Rationalizing that it was God's will to bring black heathen into contact with Christianity, even if

it meant a lifetime of enforced servitude, their ships carried slaves to labor in the Caribbean colonies as early as 1517. With the approval of their governments and the Roman Catholic Church, the sellers of flesh maintained that "christianized" slaves were better off than free heathen.[2]

Because the slave trade was so extensive and because so many of its promulgators claimed to be Christians, this religious justification had to be promoted with as little resistance as possible. And the myth of inferiority had to be valid in the minds of the slaves as well as in the minds of the white traders so they would accept it as natural.

Thus, early in the exploration and development of the New World, the capture of slaves was done under the pretext of Christianizing the slaves. Because the "savages" needed "true religion" to replace their paganism, it seemed justifiable to bring them to the New World with its strong Puritan heritage. Never mind, of course, that this "noble end" would dismantle African families, orphan African children, often destroy the continuity of African culture, and frequently make African women the victims of rape.

Sociologist Hank Allen describes the plight of these early slaves:

> They came into slavery with varying languages, cultural traditions, rituals, and kinship networks. This, along with an unfamiliarity of American geography, effectively prevented slaves from developing the kind of complex social organization, technology, and mobilization that would be necessary to alleviate their plight. . . . Moreover, to reinforce their brutal social and psychological control, slaveholders often eliminated any bonds of kinship or culture by dividing captured Africans into groups of mixed tribal origins before selling them to plantation owners.[3]

A good friend told me the story of how his great-great-grandfather, Silas Greene, who was a slave, was sold away from his family to another plantation at the age of nine. This must have been a tragic and shocking experience for a nine-year-old, to be taken from his parents for the sake of his master's financial benefit. The economics of slavery were without sensitivity, caring little that a nine-year-old child would be robbed of his mother's love and his father's counsel.

Because many Christians presumed that paganism was inherently part of the African's religion, they looked to the Bible, the sourcebook of the Christian religion, to authenticate the slave industry. Never mind that slavery based on kidnapping was clearly forbidden in Scripture, and punishable by death (Ex. 21:16). This set the stage for the infamous "curse of Ham" doctrine.[4]

The Curse of Ham

Because Ham was the father of black people, and because his descendants were cursed to be slaves because of his sin against Noah, some Christians said, "Africans and their descendants are destined to be servants, and should accept their status as slaves in fulfillment of biblical prophecy."[5]

Due to the curse of Ham theory, there now existed a myth of inferiority with apparent biblical roots. This theological basis provided the raw material necessary to convince the slaves that to resist their assigned inferior status was to resist the will of God. This myth became an authoritative one because it was rooted in a purported theology, and slave owners used this twisted belief system to sustain a perverted sociology.

I knew that something did not sound right about the curse of Ham theory when I first heard it as a teenager. A white minister was giving me the biblical reason that my people and I had to endure the humiliation of American racism. Because I couldn't prove otherwise and because my favorite Bible, the famous Scofield Reference Bible,[6] which had become the official version of American fundamentalism, endorsed the curse of Ham theory, I had little recourse other than to accept it. After all, those promoting it were "trained" in the Bible and theology at the finest fundamentalist institutions in our country—institutions, by the way, that at that time would not allow African Americans to enroll as students.

The endorsement of the Old Scofield Bible, one of the most influential reference works revered by the evangelical fundamentalist community, gave full consent to nourish the notion of a biblically sanctioned black inferiority. This, coupled with the legal status of American segregation, did nothing to ameliorate the already culturally inflicted and discolored perception of black people in the minds of white Bible students, firmly establishing and embedding the myth in the American Christian psyche. This theologically endorsed determinism gave passive sanction to the manifest destiny worldview of the superiority of the white race while simultaneously justifying the use of the Bible to seek to denigrate both the psyche and value of black people.

Never mind, of course, that the Bible says that Canaan, Ham's son, was cursed, not Ham himself. Thus, only one of Ham's four sons, not all four, was cursed. How then could all black people everywhere be cursed?

Never mind that the curse on Canaan and his descendants—"Now therefore, you are cursed, and you shall never cease being slaves"—finds its most obvious fulfillment in the ongoing defeat and subjugation of Canaan by Israel (Josh. 9:23; 1 Kings 9:20–21).

Never mind that the descendants of Ham's other sons—Cush, Mizraim, and Put—have continued to this day as national peoples in Ethiopia (Cush), Egypt (Mizraim), and Libya (Put). In fact, founders of the first two great civilizations, Sumer (Mesopotamia) and Egypt, descended from Ham.

And never mind that God says that curses based on disobedience only extend to three or four generations at most and are reversed when people repent and turn again to obedience (Ex. 20:5–6). This is certainly sufficient to negate the Christian endorsement of the American enslavement of black Christians.

Myths, however, do not need facts; they simply need supporters. Because the myth of inferiority needed as much theological support as possible to make it stick, Christians turned to the New Testament to corroborate the Old Testament verses on masters and slaves and quoted biblical passages on slaves submitting to their masters (e.g., Eph. 6:5–8; Col. 3:22) to contemporize the myth to the economic framework of the New World.

The Puritans were attempting to turn America into the "city set on a hill," the manifestation of the prophesied kingdom of God on earth. Slavery provided an economic base for implementing this theology, even among some of the theological and religious heroes of the colonial era. Some of the noted New England leaders who endorsed this perspective of slavery were George Whitefield, John Davenport, Evera Styles, and Jonathan Edwards.[7] They attempted to teach the slaves to docilely accept their inferior status, for to do so was the will of God. To fail to do so was to rebel against God and risk eternal punishment.[8]

With this comprehensive "biblical" strategy, the myth of inferiority took theological wings. These Christians forgot that the apostle Paul told masters to treat converted slaves as equal brothers in Christ (Philem. 15–16). They forgot that the apostle Paul said that slaves had the right to try to change their status (1 Cor. 7:21). And they forgot that the masters' authority over slaves was limited. It was not within the master's rights to treat a slave in an inhumane manner. Masters were to apply the Golden Rule to slaves and were not to treat them as children of a lesser god. The God who rules both heaven and earth will show no partiality to those who commit evil against mankind, whether slave or free, master or servant (Eph. 6:8–9).

The colonial Christians forgot Paul's writing to the Ephesians that says, "For He Himself is our peace, who made both groups into one and broke down the barrier of the dividing wall, by abolishing in His flesh the enmity" (Eph. 2:14–15). Barriers no longer exist between people's fellowship with God or each other, Paul said.

They forgot the biblical truth that to be members of the body of Christ means that preferences based on class, culture, or race are totally unacceptable to God, and people who make such preferences are candidates for His judgment (James 2:9–13). Such biblical data, however, would not support the inferiority myth. Adding such biblical references would be telling the whole truth, and truth and myth do not mix very well. Therefore, early Americans had to be selective about what Bible verses to use to establish a theological basis to justify slavery and perpetuate the inferiority myth.

The foundational and fundamental failure of white Christianity was its refusal to recognize the *imago Dei* that has been stamped on every human being (Gen. 1:26–28). The foundational and fundamental failure of black Christianity was to believe it. Unfortunately, the inferiority myth has been alive within the black culture itself. Martin Luther King Jr. said it best when he declared, "a man can't ride your back unless it is bent!"[9] The myth made blacks, at times, wish they were white, and it produced a path of self-destruction and character ridicule within black culture.

As a result, African Americans began to view large noses as a sign of ugliness and natural black hair as unkempt. Director and well-known actor Bill Duke reflects the honest feelings of so many young black kids growing up under this myth when he shared how at one point as a kindergartener, he tried to drink bleach in order to be white.[10] Bill shares how his parents' response to his pain of coming to terms with being black in a racist environment in the 1940s was to tell him, "You're no better than anyone else. But, also, no one else is any better than you." He says that this truth in turn helped him go on to succeed as well as he has over the last seventy years. Bill's parents sought to dig up the seeds of this myth of inferiority early on because they knew how damaging it could be.[11]

Once such mythological representations were made, it was easy to justify laws to enforce the myth. Consider the infamous Dred Scott decision of 1857, which ruled that black people were not US citizens, but instead were property to be bought, sold, or killed at the whims of their masters. It wrongly divided the word of truth, as God's Holy Word was used as a tool to justify slavery, segregation, and racial violence in order for whites to maintain and advance an evil racial, political, and economic superiority.

Not until the black revolution of the sixties did African Americans corporately reject the inferiority myth, although blacks had attempted to discredit the myth throughout black history. With all of America watching, African Americans categorically rejected the shackles of second-class citizenship and made a progressive push for inclusion. During this period the media became a friend, rather than a foe, as the black case for equality controlled the national debate and demonstrated graphically how debased the superiority myth had become. Laws began to change, opportunities began to come, enhancement programs were established, and massive amounts of funds were allocated and spent. All were designed to appear to address the myth once and for all. Whether they accomplished that, or were simply lip service set to inept policies, is a discussion for another day.

American culture is still reeling from the effects of the inferiority myth. Although the African American church has its own distinctive and valuable appeal, Christian whites often presume that the brand of Christianity that comes through the broader evangelical community is the most significant vehicle of Christianity in America. In sociological studies, this is termed "whiteness as normative." It is where life is viewed from the starting point of white culture, and everything else is held up to it as the standard or is to be viewed through that lens.

Even in the late 1980s, I was being told by "evangelical" radio stations that blacks in broadcasting might be too offensive to the broader Christian community. The white preacher was normative, and to air anyone different would disrupt this status quo. As in other arenas of life, I was hearing again that blacks could be consumers of the Christian faith from the broader Christian community but could not expect to be producers of Christian ministry for the church at large. This attitude also explains why white Christian groups quickly call upon Christian blacks to join them in their outreach ministries, such as evangelistic crusades, family worship, or anti-abortion rallies, but they are slow to respond when Christian blacks call upon them for their involvement in the justice concerns of the black church and black community. Any invitations of unity usually implied Christian blacks unifying in support of the agenda of the white church, but rarely worked the other way.

Lincoln and Mamiya, authors of *The Black Church in the African American Experience*, are correct when they state:

> The prevailing American sentiment has traditionally held that the mainline white churches constitute the only relevant spiritual pulse in the nation, and that whatever is outside this narrow ambit is of little if any significance to the American religious profile. This conventional wisdom is widely reflected in seminary curricula and denominational policies to the end that misperception is compounded, and the religious experience of some 30 to 35 million African Americans is clouded in consequence.[12]

Generally, the tendency is to dismiss African American worship and church practices as something that is purely cultural and void of any significant spiritual or theological fiber. The black church member is often viewed as an emotionalist, rather than someone who has a deep, authentic understanding and appreciation of God. Those who peer in from the outside have little or no access to the essence of African American church life and are worse off because of it. Until there is a willingness on behalf of whites in the evangelical world to sit or serve underneath the leadership and teaching of blacks, and not simply drop in from time to time for a "cultural" experience, true racial progress will not have been achieved.

Yet, just as "whites gain superiority by not knowing blacks; blacks gain entitlement by not seeing their own responsibility for bettering themselves."[13] White guilt, coupled with black power, continuously feed off each other, keeping both groups in an illegitimate bondage of negative mutual dependence. Such an unholy alliance can never resolve our continuous racial calamity because it keeps both groups caged in unhealthy worldviews. "For persons who see themselves as victims," writes John Perkins, "it is easy to be ensnared by pride. We can carry our pain as a badge of honor and try to whip others with it. . . . This pride can easily slide into a feeling of entitlement. That I'm owed something."[14]

Once a person realizes his unique position in divine history, however, he begins to realize that no person or racial group has the final say about another person's or group's potential. This realization is by far the greatest need in black America today, and unless it occurs, no amount of "race-hustling" or political protest will reverse the situation a large segment of African Americans now face. A comprehensive understanding of a kingdom agenda view on race and oppression, a Kingdom Race Theology (which I talk about in my booklet by that name), leaves no room for the embracing of victimology, even if you are being victimized. The Bible clearly teaches that God's children have been given all that we need through the power of the Holy Spirit to overcome, rather than succumb to, opposition and oppression. As former civil rights leader Robert Woodson said recently, "It's really white supremacy to assume that blacks have no agency,"[15] which is what the victim-only ideology perpetuates.

Acknowledging how tough the journey to improvement and betterment is remains a valid part of overcoming opposition. But instead of spending too much time seeking to place blame, we must also look for and operate out of the strengths God has given us. Racism is real and evil, making the battle before us a difficult one. However, too much of an unhealthy focus on racism and white guilt will keep us bound to both and keep African Americans in an ongoing state of dependency wherein the "oppressor" defines our existence as the "oppressed." It is like the Dallas Cowboys focusing so much on the eleven men on the other side of the ball that they neglect to implement plays on how to move past them. The idea is to go through, around, and over the opposing forces against you.

To begin this process, both Christian blacks and whites must demythologize the myth of inferiority so the mental fog that clouds the racial atmosphere can be removed. Both will then be free to relate to each other on our mutual strengths, derived from the biblically based understanding of our heritage as it is rooted and grounded in the God "from whom every family in heaven and on earth derives its name" (Eph. 3:15).

It has been my desire over the past five decades of professional ministry as a black man in America to be one of many biblical thinkers who help dispel the inferiority myth that has impacted not only the racial groups of our country, but individuals as well. Each of us is held hostage to the perspectives of our racial group, thus limiting our personal development and our ability to work toward racial harmony and oneness in our nation and, most importantly, in the body of Christ.

Unless biblical Christians significantly enter the fray and take over the leadership for unifying the racial divide, we will be hopelessly deadlocked in a sea of relativity regarding this issue, resulting in re-stating more questions rather than providing permanent answers.

It is my uncompromising contention that the only proper perspective is the divine perspective; the only proper agenda is the kingdom agenda, not an American political one. If the Bible is allowed to be the standard by which blacks and whites determine truth, then freedom from this moral and racial malaise will be the outcome; for as Jesus taught, the truth has a unique capacity for making people free.

Only when we define ourselves and see our relationships in light of the absolute authority of Scripture and the overarching rule of God in our lives can we begin to place salve on the open wounds that have kept America in general and Christians in particular in a perpetual state of disunity.

Chapter 3

The Black Presence in the Bible

Egyptology and the study of African history and culture are beginning to highlight, now more than ever, the unique role black people have played in the development of the human race, world civilizations, and in the narratives of the Bible. Anthropologists of all races are grappling with the increasing plausibility that the roots of human civilization are in Africa with black people.[1] The Rev. Walter McCray, author of *The Black Presence in the Bible*, wrote,

> The preponderance of contemporary evidence being gathered by archaeologists and ancient historians says that Africa (in Egypt's Nile Valley) was the origination of humanity and civilization. It was from here that humanity, an indigenous "Black" humanity, had its beginnings. The preponderance of archaeological and historical facts say that the roots of all people are in Africa!—Egypt, Africa!
>
> Whether one holds to the traditional view of a Mesopotamian origination of humanity, or to the more substantiated view of the origination of humanity in Africa, one

51

point of harmony is certain: indigenous humanity and the originators of the civilizations in each of these areas were Black! They were Black in Egyptian Africa and they were Black in Asia's lower Mesopotamia! Either way one cuts it, the originators of civilization were a Black people.[2]

Such evidence includes the discoveries in the Tanzanian Canyon of the Olduvai Gorge, which reveals that toolmaking began in Africa and then spread to Europe. It includes the discoveries in the Nile Valley that demonstrate that people of Negroid African descent manufactured pottery before pottery was made in the world's oldest known city. Archaeological evidence even suggests African sailors explored the New World prior to Columbus. This evidence includes an extensive number of portraits of Negroes on clay, gold, and stone unearthed in pre-Columbian strata in Central and South America. In fact, paintings by Negro people date prior to 3000 BC.

"Civilization started in the great river valleys of Africa and Asia, in the Fertile Crescent in the Near East and along the narrow ribbon of the Nile in Africa," says historian Lerone Bennett. "In the Nile Valley that beginning was an African as well as an Asian achievement. Blacks, or people who would be considered blacks today, were among the first people to use tools, paint pictures, plant seeds and worship gods."[3] Bennett's conclusion concurs with Moses' assertion that Adam was created from soil in or near the land of Cush, who was Ham's son and originator of the great Ethiopian civilization (Gen. 2:7, 13; 10:6, 8; see also Isa. 18:1–2).

For African Americans this knowledge is both a great strength and a great weakness. The obvious strength is the very real self-appreciation of the depth of our historical achievements and contributions. Finally scholars, both black and white, are correcting the inaccuracies and deletions that have been taught by many people who have bypassed the truth, by either the sin of omission or commission. We now have the academic tools necessary to refute those who relegate blacks to an inferior status in history and who use erroneous theological, environmental, or cultural arguments to support their perspective that whites are superior to blacks.[4]

On the other hand, black people, particularly Christian blacks, must filter black achievement, history, and culture through the lens of Scripture in order to see it clearly. Greatness must be defined in terms of biblical criteria, not in terms of simple social theory.

THE NEED FOR A BIBLICAL
PERSPECTIVE OF BLACK PEOPLES

I prefer to look to the Bible for an understanding of who I am as an African American. The Bible is the inerrant, infallible, authoritative Word of God; it is the only place we can go to receive a totally accurate and objective understanding of race. Whites and blacks alike have used and misused race for their own advantages. Both races have allowed popular opinion, sociopolitical structures, cultural traditions, and personal preferences to "color" their views about themselves and others.

During the era of slavery whites viewed themselves more highly than others in an attempt to persuade blacks to view ourselves more lowly than others. On the other hand, during the sixties revolution black pride was sometimes taken to violent extremes. The Bible does not suffer from such human lopsidedness because its author is God, and God gives the truth on who we are, whose we are, and how we ought to think of ourselves (Rom. 12:3).

Rooting racial history and culture in the Bible allows us to contradict blacks who write off the Bible as a white man's book and Christianity as a white man's religion. When a person understands the glorious presence of African people in God's drama of redemptive history, Scripture is clearly the primary source for legitimate black pride. Those who reject the Bible stand on shaky racial ground. The Scripture allows blacks to take pride in who we are and what God has made us, without feeling we have to become something other than what God created us to be.

Race has played a major role in the social development and the functioning of American society. It benefits us to discover God's perspective of racial prejudice. Moses faced racial prejudice when his sister, Miriam, and brother, Aaron, challenged his God-given leadership because he was married to an African woman, a Cushite (Num. 12:1). What apparently bothered them was not simply that Moses' new bride was dark-complexioned, because it has been proven that other Israelites were also dark-skinned. Rather, it was that she was black and foreign. Her African ethnic origin was unacceptable. It is important to note here that God punished Miriam with the disease of leprosy for her rebellion against Moses "because of the Cushite woman whom he had married." God turned Miriam's skin white, causing her to be "leprous, as white as snow" (Num. 12:10).

Racism, whether based on skin color or ethnicity, has always been a terrible sin in the eyes of God and worthy of His severest judgment. However, such judgment can be reversed when repentance takes place (vv. 11–15). Both white and black people who allow race to determine social and political structures in America need to remember that.

It is clear from Scripture that black people are objects of God's love and grace. The very lineage of Jesus included blacks, and Africans were among the leaders of the first-century church. Thus, African Americans and white Americans can see that black people are an integral part of God's redemptive agenda and have played a decisive role in disseminating that kingdom agenda to the rest of the world. All Christians need to understand the eternal dimensions of black history.[5]

The Bible is our common ground. It is the guidebook that links black and white Christians to God's eternal truth. Therefore we should look to it for an understanding of race relations, just as we read it to know how to make our everyday decisions.

The Bible is the primary source for legitimate racial pride, self-authentication, self-analysis, intracultural and cross-cultural analysis, and determining God's view of a group's national purpose. The Bible alone fulfills this function with honesty and integrity and should be the starting point for any group to find out its true identity. A biblical perspective is crucial if black people are going to relate properly to their roots and if white people are going to better understand and see us for who we are.

Most black churches celebrate Black History Month, but the focus is usually on black American history because there is very little awareness or appreciation for black biblical history. However, part of the process of discipleship within the black church as well as the white church needs to be to equip our congregations by providing biblical, historically accurate, and logical answers to the relevance and value of the ancestral presence of blacks in Scripture. Without it, African Americans are asked to define ourselves with an inaccurate view of our place in history. Anytime people have an incomplete view of themselves, it affects their actions, thus perpetuating many preconceived notions of perception and identification.

THE BIBLE AND BLACK PEOPLE

Voluminous attention is given throughout the Bible to the issues of race, culture, genealogy, and geography as they relate to the identification of groups of people. There is no such thing as cultural or racial neutrality. Every person belongs to some group. Even when groups intermingle, they either lean toward identification with one culture or the other, or they synthesize into a totally new group (such as the Samaritans, who were the offspring of Jewish and Assyrian intermarrying).

There is really only one race: the human race (Acts 17:26). All humans stem from one root: Adam and Eve. Yet within the human race there are varieties of individuals and ethnicities. One of the ways we distinguish between individuals and groups is by color.

Likewise, the Bible defines individuals and groups of people by color. Yet the biblical definitions are unencumbered by the negative distortions and reactions that have historically been associated with blackness in American society.

When discussing the issue of blacks in the Bible, we must understand that the designation "black" is a term of accommodation. We are using a twenty-first-century mindset to discuss people who, in some cases, lived more than two millennia ago. Our distinctions are not necessarily their distinctions. For example, the Romans made a distinction between people who were dark-skinned and people who had Negroid physiognomy. Today both groups would be considered black.

When we say "black" in reference to those peoples of the past, we are, on the one hand, referring to the physical traits African Americans share with those ancient peoples, namely skin color. On the other hand, we are referring to the genetic lineage of African Americans and its affinity with peoples of the ancient Near East and Egypt.

There is no question that dark-complexioned people played a prominent role in biblical events. Descendants of African peoples have, beyond a doubt, an ancestral link to certain critical personages in biblical history.

We are sure of this because the color black is used in the Bible to refer to the skin tone of any dark-complexioned people from African or Hamitic descent. Such a descriptive use of color can be found in the actual names of persons, people groups, and places, particularly in the Old Testament world.

In biblical times, the names parents gave their children described their hopes for the child or the circumstances surrounding the child. When Rachel was dying in childbirth, she called her son Ben-oni, "son of my sorrow" (Gen. 35:18). Biblical people used descriptive names to relate their experiences at certain locations. Marah, which means "bitter," received its name because of the bitterness of the waters located there (Ex. 15:23).

Names also reflected the character or action of a person. Nabal was like his name; he was a "fool" (1 Sam. 25:25). Names were even changed when there was a need for a new description of a person, place, or relationship. Jacob was renamed Israel (Gen. 32:27; 35:10). Jesus changed Simon's name to Peter, "the stone." Thus, biblical names are akin to our contemporary use of nicknames; they are used to describe some characteristic of a person.

Names also referred to the actual skin tone of dark-complexioned people. For example, *kedar* means "to be dark,"[6] thus, Kedarites are a dark-skinned people (Gen. 25:13; Ps. 120:5). *Phinehas* means "the Negro" or "Nubian," who were a dark-skinned people (Ex. 6:25; 1 Chron. 9:20). According to Exodus 6:25, Phinehas was the son of Eleazar and his wife, who was a daughter of Putiel. This is interesting, because when Phinehas was born, Israel was already established as a separate commonwealth, although it was in transit. Therefore, at least some of the citizens within the commonwealth of Israel were giving birth to children whose names characterized them as Nubian or Negroes. Thus the children of Israel must have been heterogeneous.

It is important to remember that the claim to the inheritance of Jacob was not a matter of skin color, but instead a matter of lineage. The critical question was, "Who was your father?" not "What color is your skin?" It is also important to remember that Manasseh and Ephraim were born to Joseph while he was in Egypt. Yet Jacob (Israel) made it very clear in Genesis 48:5 that Manasseh and Ephraim were to be treated as though they were Jacob's sons; therefore they were to receive an inheritance in the promised land. Nubian genetics definitely entered the line of Israel at this juncture, if not before.

Perhaps Putiel's name provides us with an understanding of who his people were. The first three letters of Putiel's name appear to have a lexical/etymological link to Put, one of the sons of Ham.[7] Where the name Put is used in the Old Testament, it usually names African peoples (Jer. 46:9; Ezek. 27:10; 30:5; 38:5). This would certainly explain how Phinehas was born a Nubian in the midst of a Semitic congregation.

Furthermore, a total of seventy people from Jacob's family entered Egypt (Gen. 46:27). Yet the Bible says that some six hundred thousand men alone came out of Egypt with Moses (Ex. 12:37). The total number involved in the Exodus, including women and children, is estimated to be more than two million. Marriages to Egyptian women, much like those of Joseph and Eleazar, would have produced dark-skinned offspring such as Phinehas.

Jeremiah 43:7 refers to the place called Tahpanhes, which means "palace of the Negro." The name Ham means "hot" or "heat." The name is an implicit association or reference to burnt or dark skin, especially since he was the progenitor of African peoples,[8] and also because the names of his brothers reflected their skin tone as well; Shem means "dusky," and Japheth means "fair."

Another name associated with color is Simeon, "who was called Niger" (Acts 13:1). A *Greek-English Lexicon of the New Testament* comments on Simeon's nickname in this way: "Niger (dark-complexioned), surname of Simeon the prophet."[9]

As I mentioned earlier, Moses' wife identified in Numbers 12:1 is one of the Cushites, a group of African people coming from the region south of Egypt and characterized with black skin.[10]

The Shulamite bride of King Solomon twice describes her complexion as black (Song 1:5–6). Of special note here is the spirit of legitimate pride associated with her recognition of her color, for she saw herself as black and beautiful.

Jeremiah, likewise, recognized people in terms of color when he raised the question, "Can the Ethiopian change his skin?" (Jer. 13:23). Jeremiah said that black skin color was as basic to the Ethiopian as unrighteous behavior was to the nation Israel. It was a permanent characteristic.

A BASIS FOR BLACK PRIDE IN THE BIBLE

Because all humanity has its origin in Adam and the three sons of Noah (Gen. 9:18–19; Acts 17:26), this is an appropriate starting point for gaining a proper biblical basis for racial identity. And because we all stem from the same root, it is absurd for any group to claim superiority over another. It was God's intention to reestablish the human race through the three sons of Noah; therefore, God legitimized all races over which each son stands as head and over which Noah presides as father. This is especially true since the Scripture says that God blessed Noah and his sons, and the command to repopulate the earth was comprehensive and equally applied to each of them (Gen. 9:1).

Each son is associated with nations of peoples, as is recorded in the Table of Nations in Genesis 10.[11] Black people, then, as all other races, can take pride in the fact that it was God's intention that we exist, survive, and function as nations of peoples.

One particularly informative verse is 1 Chronicles 4:40, which indicates that Hamitic people living in Canaan positively contributed to community life, productivity, and social well-being: "They found rich and good pasture, and the land was broad and quiet and peaceful; for those who lived there formerly were Hamites." Here, we have a biblical foundation for appropriately placed black pride.

When one examines the biblical data, it becomes distinctively clear that black people have an awesome heritage.

INFLUENTIAL BLACKS IN THE BIBLE

The Sons of Ham

Noah's son Ham had four sons: Cush, Mizraim, Put, and Canaan. Cush was the progenitor of the Ethiopian people. This is validated by the fact that the names Cush and Ethiopia are used interchangeably in the Scriptures (Gen. 2:13; 10:6). Mizraim was the progenitor of the Egyptian people, who are understood in Scripture to have been a Hamitic people, and thus African (Pss. 78:51; 105:23, 26–27; 106:21–22). Put was the progenitor of Libya, and Canaan was the progenitor of the Canaanites, one of the most problematic foes of God's chosen people, the Israelites.

Nimrod

Of particular importance is the powerful Old Testament figure Nimrod, the descendant of Cush, who ruled in the land of Shinar (Gen. 10:8–10; 11:2). Nimrod eventually became the father of two of the greatest empires in the Bible and in world history, Assyria and Babylonia. He was the first great leader of a world civilization (Gen. 10:10–12). He led all the people on earth and served as earth's protector. Nimrod's presence and accomplishments confirm the unique and early leadership role black people played in world history, albeit not always in a spiritually beneficial way (Gen. 11:1–9).

The Tribe of Ephraim

Hamitic peoples were crucial to the program of God throughout Old Testament biblical history. Joseph's wife, an Egyptian[12] woman (Gen. 41:45, 50–52), was the mother of Manasseh and Ephraim, who later became leaders of Jewish tribes. In fact, the tribe of Ephraim produced one of the greatest leaders Israel ever had—Moses' successor, Joshua (Num. 13:8; 1 Chron. 7:22–27). This Jewish-African link is very strong in Scripture. The prophet Amos said, "Are you not as the sons of Ethiopia to Me, O sons of Israel?' declares the Lord" (Amos 9:7).

Caleb

Caleb was the son of Jephunneh the Kennizzite; the Kennizzites were a part of the Canaanite tribes (Gen. 15:19) and descendants of Ham. Caleb also came from the tribe of Judah (Josh. 14:6, 14). Judah, the progenitor of the tribe, fathered twin sons by Tamar, a Hamitic woman (Gen. 38). Caleb joined with Joshua as one of the two spies who went to explore Canaan and brought back a positive report to enter the land and take possession of it, as God had declared (Num. 13–14).

Jethro

Jethro, Moses' father-in-law, from whom Moses received the greatest single piece of advice regarding national leadership, ministry organization, political strategy, and personal planning ever recorded (Ex. 18:13–27), was a Kenite (Judg. 1:16), part of the Canaanite tribes who descended from Ham (Gen. 15:19). At that time, the Kenites had settled in the land of Midian.

Another interesting observation regarding Jethro is that he is identified as "the priest of Midian" (Ex. 3:1). Since he was a priest, yet he was not a Levite and the Aaronic priesthood had not yet been established, the question is: What kind of priesthood could this have been? The only other priesthood within the framework of Scripture to which Jethro could have belonged was the priesthood of Melchizedek (Gen. 14:18). This is significant because Christ was a priest after the order of Melchizedek (Heb. 7:17). This means that the priest Jethro, who was of African descent, may have been indicative of pre-Aaronic priesthoods, such as that of Melchizedek, which foreshadowed the priestly role of both Christ and the church.

This, then, is another basis for recognizing the strategic role Africans played in the biblical saga that continues today, because all Christians are related to Jethro and his priesthood as part of the royal priesthood.

Zipporah

Zipporah was the daughter of Jethro, the African wife of Moses. She bore him two sons and rescued his life from divine judgment when she circumcised her son—a task that belonged to Moses (Ex. 2:21–22; 4:24–26; 18:2–3). If she is the same black wife of Moses spoken of in Numbers, then God intervened on her behalf against the racism regarding their interracial marriage by Moses' brother and sister (Num. 12:1–15).

Ebed-Melech

Ebed-Melech was a godly royal black African official in the palace of King Zedekiah of Judah during the time of the siege of Jerusalem. His name means "servant of the King." He was used by God to assist the prophet Jeremiah in his release from prison when Jeremiah had been sentenced to death. Ebed-Melech was rewarded for his heroism with the divine message that he would not fall by the sword during the fall of Jerusalem to the Babylonians because of his trust in God (Jer. 38:1–13; 39:15–18).

Simon of Cyrene

Simon of Cyrene, who helped Jesus on the Via Dolorosa, was of African descent. This we know because Cyrene is a country in North Africa (Matt. 27:32). He was compelled by the Romans to carry the cross of Christ to His crucifixion site. This means that the first person to follow behind Jesus, bear His cross, and have Christ's blood run off on him was a black man. This is the spiritual posture of discipleship

God calls all believers to have as we identify with Christ and His suffering (Matt. 27:32; Mark 15:21; Luke 23:26).

David

King David is known not only as a man after God's own heart (1 Sam. 13:14) but as one of the greatest kings in Israel's history. David's great-grandmother was a Canaanite woman, Rahab, who is also listed in the Hall of Faith (Heb. 11:31). David's grandmother was Ruth, a Moabite, from a people who were Canaanites as well. David, one of the heroes of the faith, hailed from mixed Jewish and Hamitic ancestry and stands as a leader of whom blacks can be proud to call our own.

Solomon

Solomon was David's son with Bathsheba, a Hamitic woman. Bathsheba literally means the daughter of Sheba. The Table of Nations identifies Sheba in the line of Ham, making Sheba a descendant from an African nation (Gen. 10:7). The Song of Solomon describes Solomon's features as "tanned and handsome, better than ten thousand others! His head is purest gold, and he has wavy, raven hair" (Song 5:10–11 TLB). Solomon was not only the wisest man to rule a nation, but he also brought about the greatest extension of Israel's reach as a kingdom (1 Kings 3:3–14). Solomon's great-great-grandmother, great-grandmother, and mother gave him roots within the black race, and place him as an example of black achievement.

Zephaniah

Underscoring the fact that black people are an integral part of God's revelatory process in both the proclamation and recording of divine revelation is the prophet Zephaniah.

The Old Testament states that Zephaniah was of Hamitic origin. He was from the lineage of Cush (Zeph. 1:1), and he prophesied

God's judgment on Judah and her enemies for their rebellion against God and their gross idolatry; yet, he proclaimed, the grace of God would save a remnant and restore blessing to the people.

People of African descent can take pride in God's prophet Zephaniah, one of the biblical authors, as their forefather.

Simeon and Lucius

The church at Antioch had two black men as leaders. Their names were Simeon, who was called Niger or black (as I mentioned earlier), and Lucius, who was from Cyrene. These two black men assisted in the ordination and commissioning of the apostle Paul (Acts 13:1–3). This verifies that black people were not only leaders in the culture of the New Testament era, but also leaders in the church itself.

The Ethiopian Eunuch

The Ethiopian eunuch is most likely responsible for the establishment or expansion of the Coptic church in a large part of Africa. While, according to tradition, Mark the Evangelist was one of the first to bring the gospel to Alexandria in Egypt where the Coptic branch of Christianity began to develop and spread, the Ethiopian eunuch carried the seed of Christianity into East Africa.

This talented man revealed the high degree of organizational and administrative responsibility that existed within the upper echelons of Ethiopian culture. The Bible describes him as a eunuch of great authority under "Candace, queen of the Ethiopians, who was in charge of all her treasure" (Acts 8:27). According to the standard Greek lexical studies, the word *Ethiopian* is of Greek origin. It literally means "burnt face."[13] The term *eunuch* does not necessarily denote emasculation; it can refer to high military and political officials.[14]

The scriptural account of the Ethiopian official is significant for two reasons. First, it acknowledges the existence of a kingdom of dark-skinned peoples at the time of first-century Christianity.

Second, it records the continuation of Christianity in Africa after having been initiated through the first African-Jewish proselytes who were converts at Pentecost (Acts 2:10). This account of Philip's encounter with the Ethiopian official verifies God's promise in Zephaniah 3:9–10: "For then I will give to the peoples purified lips, that all of them may call on the name of the LORD, to serve Him shoulder to shoulder. From beyond the rivers of Ethiopia My worshipers, My dispersed ones, will bring My offerings."

These verses show God's desire: He wishes to call to Himself peoples from the African continent, not into servitude and disdain as some incorrectly surmise, but into brotherhood with all men to serve Him "shoulder to shoulder."

As we see in history, the Ethiopian eunuch's influence has reached generations and transformed an entire culture for Christ. According to tradition, current Ethiopia was once the powerful kingdom of Axum. Its king, Ezaha, became one of the first world rulers to make Christianity the official religion of his kingdom, which became a major center for the faith. When Marco Polo visited Ethiopia, he referred to it as a magnificent Christian land. In 1173, Ethiopians were hosted by a gathering of church leaders in Constantinople. Between 1200–1500 the Zagwe dynasty ruled the land and led an expansion of the church. One of them, Zara Yaqob, worked to purge Ethiopia of traditional African religion. By the 1480s, the Church of Santo Stefano degli Abissini was built in Rome specifically for the use of Ethiopian visitors and settlers. Since the Ethiopian church wasn't the product of European influences, it developed its own distinct religious customs and a slightly different canon of Scripture. To this day, the Ethiopian church carries forward these distinctives.

Blacks in the Lineage of Christ

Deserving of our greatest attention is the lineage of Christ. Over and over again, the prophets prophesied that the Messiah would come from the seed of David. As we have already seen, the Davidic line finds a number of black people within it. Of the five women mentioned in Matthew's genealogy (Matt. 1:1–16), four are of Hamitic descent—Tamar, Rahab, Bathsheba, and Ruth.

The point here is not that Jesus was black. To assert such, as some black theologians and religious leaders do, is to fall into the exclusionist perspective of many whites who would make Jesus an Anglo-European, blue-eyed blond who had very little relevance to people of color. It would also fail to respect the distinct Jewish heritage of Christ. Rather, Jesus was mestizo—a person of mixed ancestry.

It blesses me to know that Jesus had black in His blood, because this destroys any perception of black inferiority once and for all. In Christ we find perfect man and sinless Savior. In Christ, we all have our heritage.

Black people, as all other people, can find a place of historical, cultural, and racial identity in Him. As Savior of all mankind, He can relate to all people, in every situation. In Him, any person from any background can find comfort, understanding, direction, and affinity, as long as He is revered as the Son of God, a designation that transcends every culture and race and one to which all nations of people must pay homage.

Even when we leave the pages of the New Testament era, we run into African people of the faith who had a profound influence upon the expansion of Christianity.

THE CHURCH FATHERS

For centuries church fathers, anointed men of erudition, have sculpted the development of the Christian faith and have postulated ways to articulate the deep and intricate truths of Christian theology. A great disservice has been done to people of African descent in the failure of church historians to identify the African, Hamitic descent of many of the most noted church fathers. By looking at the strategic place black African people have played in the history and development of the Christian faith, both through their piety and intellectual prowess exercised for the glory of God, we authenticate God's continual activity in the black race. We also encourage Christians of African descent to see ourselves as the continuation of a divine legacy. Our opulent heritage should serve to motivate us to continue dispensing God's truth by means of the talents He has deposited in our community, not only for the benefit of the black community in particular but also for the Christian community at large.

Augustine, who was by far the most scholarly and influential of all the church fathers, has influenced our church fathers from his teachings. The greater majority of his doctrinal conclusions have stood the test of time and the scrutiny of many theologians throughout the annals of theological history. Upon observing his life experience through the lens of his *Confessions*, one can easily see his strong view of the grace of God. The thought and contribution of Augustine became the theological foundation for the Protestant Reformation as well as contemporary Reformed Calvinistic theology.

Augustine's words and thoughts are studied in Bible schools and seminaries. He is known as the Father of Theologians and also referred to as the "father of orthodox theology." However, it is often left out that he was not only African, but also most probably was black.[15] We know this because his mother, Monica, was a Berber, and Berbers were a group of dark-skinned people belonging to the vicinity of Carthage.[16]

Athanasius of Alexandria was another prominent church father, theologian, statesman, and Egyptian leader. As a young man he served as secretary to Alexander, Bishop of Alexandria. Upon the death of Alexander, it was made known to Athanasius that he had been chosen by Alexander to succeed him as bishop of Alexandria. Athanasius was involved in the theological war against the heresy of Arius and the

Arians, who taught that Jesus Christ was not truly God, but a lesser creature. It was because of this heresy that the Council of Nicaea met in the year AD 325, and Athanasius welcomed the definition of the Son that stated He was "consubstantial with the Father."

Like Augustine, Athanasius' words and thoughts are taught in Bible schools and seminaries. He was known as the "black dwarf" because of his dark skin and short stature, a name he was given by his many enemies.[17] Athanasius was exiled five times by four Roman emperors and spent seventeen of the forty-five years he served as bishop of Alexandria in exile. However, he exhibited a cogent understanding of theological issues that was far beyond his own time.[18]

Quintus Septimius Florens Tertullian (c. 160–c. 225), who like Augustine lived in Carthage, was another of the great African church fathers. He is known in church history as the father of Latin theology because he was the first church leader to write his works in Latin. While it is unclear as to his precise skin tone, there is great evidence to support that he was black. He was of Berber and Phoenician origin, and Berbers were a group of dark-skinned people dominating North Africa.

Tertullian received a good education in literature and rhetoric, was trained in Greek and Latin, and became a lawyer. He converted to Christianity some time prior to AD 197, retaining skills in rhetoric and argumentation that impacted the religious environment of his day. Among his greatest contributions to Christian theology were his thoughts toward the foundation of the Trinitarian formula, often receiving credit as the first to use the word "trinity" to describe the Godhead. His notable writings include *Ad Martyras* ("To the Martyrs"), *Ad Nationes* ("To the Nations"), *Apologeticum* ("Defense"), *Adversus Marcionem* ("Against Marcion"), *Adversus Hermogenem* ("Against Hermogenes"), *Adversus Valentinianos* ("Against Valentinus"), and *De Praescriptione Haereticorum* ("Concerning the Prescription of Heretics"). From a historical perspective, Tertullian is known less for what he did than for what he wrote. In his *Prescriptions Against the Heretics* he argued that the heretics of his day had no right to refute the church and that Scripture was the sole property of the church.[19]

It should be evident from even a limited understanding of the Bible that many people of African descent have had a major role in the development and dissemination of the Christian faith. Far from being an uninformed people who were afterthoughts in the mind and plan of God, blacks were a well-informed, progressive, productive, and influential people—so much so that we were at the very center of every aspect of God's activity in history. It is only because people have failed to present an accurate reflection of historical truth that this reality is ignored.

I invite Anglos to see African Americans through the lens of Scripture rather than that of culture. In so doing, there can be a basis of equality in relationship building. If we who are black will see ourselves through the same lens of Scripture, we will discover an appropriate basis for racial pride in the God of the Bible. It also means we can give other races the same significance and respect as part of God's creation that we desire to receive from them.

Chapter 4

The Black Church's Link with Africa

My ancestors, like those of most black Americans, were brought to this country against their will from the west coast of Africa to serve as slave labor for the economic development of the New World. My great-grandparents worked the land of the South to help America uncover the vast wealth that she had been granted by God. Like virtually all Africans brought to these shores, my ancestors had to endure the agony and shame of American slavery. They were viewed as less than human, savages, thus giving sanction to the abuse and misuse of the legal system of slavery.

The fact that my African ancestors were primarily perceived by whites as savages in need of civilizing gave rise to one of the most inhumane systems of injustice ever to be perpetrated against human beings. It is a system that we are still seeking to recover from today.

My great-grandparents did not come to America from a dark and uncivilized continent. To the contrary, they were forced from their homeland where they lived with personal freedom and dignity and were brought to a country where they could be bought and sold at auction like cattle.

THE MISPERCEPTION OF AFRICA

Africa! When we hear that word, we may see images of a land untouched by the marvels of modernization. According to the typical Western mindset, Africa is a land rich in raw materials—ivory, gold, oil, and coal. To be sure, at one time the African himself was viewed as a very valuable commodity. Certainly, the African was not valued for his or her intellectual prowess.

Such a mindset spawns men like German scholar Leo Frobenius, who said,

> Before the introduction of a genuine faith and a higher standard of culture by the Arabs, the natives had neither political organization, nor, strictly spoken, any religion. . . . Therefore it is necessary, in examining the pre-Mahommedan conditions of the negro races, to confine ourselves to the description of their crude fetishism, their brutal and often cannibal customs, their vulgar and repulsive idols. . . . None but the most primitive instincts determine the lives and conduct of the negroes, who lack every kind of ethical inspiration.[1]

Only by correcting the misconceptions about the African continent can we correct the negative perception that many people have toward black people in our contemporary society, and the negative way many of us view ourselves.

It is necessary, then, to look at some key facets of African culture and religion without the impairment of Western stereotypes. By Western stereotypes I mean the cadre of beliefs and images that the Western world embraces regarding Africans and people of African descent as portrayed in the first few minutes of the evening news. In place of an in-depth view of African culture and its strengths, the West adopted a superficial and degrading assessment based on thirty-second clips of starving children, crime, and poverty that were showcased on our network television stations for decades before the onset of social media.

This propensity on the part of Europe and its satellites to look down on non-European cultures, focusing primarily on their struggles, has caused the Western world to remain in the relational "dark ages." In addition, because European colonialism has often brought with it the advent of Christianity into diverse places of the world, many non-Europeans assess Christianity through the merits of the ones bearing it. Many potential Christian converts link Christianity with a worldview of America formed through a missiological foundation often rooted in colonial sociocultural norms along with the exportation of soap operas, trashy talk shows, and questionable musical artists, and thus form a negative assessment of Jesus Christ and His salvation.

Furthermore, a narrow view of Africa leads to broad generalizations such as the trend toward fetishism (the worship of objects understood to have magical powers, such as idols), which is actually a universal trend and not limited to those in Africa. Scripture verifies this universal trend toward idolatry in Romans 1:22–23: "Professing to be wise, they became fools, and exchanged the glory of the incorruptible God for an image in the form of corruptible man and of birds and four-footed animals and crawling creatures."

Even a cursory walk through the New Testament reveals many horrid practices among the peoples of the northern coast of the Mediterranean and the area of Asia Minor under Greek influence to whom Paul wrote his letters.

In the Greek city of Corinth, people worshiped many deities, including the goddess Aphrodite. Known as Venus to the Romans, this goddess was said to have beauty that made the wise witless.[2] The worship of Aphrodite was centered around the temple erected in her honor. The liturgy involved sexual contact with the temple priestesses, that is, prostitutes. So enraptured were the Corinthians with this vile practice that the Athenian dramatist Aristophanes (ca. 450–388 BC) coined the word *korinthiazomai* (which means "to act like a Corinthian: to commit fornication").[3]

Addressing this aspect of Corinthian life in his commentary, Gordon Fee mentioned the Asclepius room in the present museum in Corinth, which he called "mute evidence of this facet of city life."[4] On a large wall stood a number of clay votives (objects given in fulfillment of a vow or pledge) of human genitals that had been offered to the god for the healing of that part of the body, which was apparently ravaged by venereal disease.

Of course, we have always been taught that venereal disease made it to Europe through Columbus's sailors, who had sex with the native women of the West Indies, which is another great Western myth. In Corinth we have evidence that venereal disease existed in Europe for at least 1,400 years before Columbus was born.

Generally, the Western world fails to acknowledge that the staple of Western society, Christianity, is non-Western. Neither Christianity nor Judaism is indigenous to Europe; rather, they are Middle Eastern in origin. Only via the prompting of the Holy Spirit and the military oppression of the Romans did Europe obtain the prize of Christianity. It was by no craving for virtue and ethical inspiration on Europe's part. However, both Christians and non-Christians often look to Christianity as the white man's religion, and because of this, some Africans have called others to return to their traditional beliefs.[5] Although I cannot in any way endorse a shift away from the Christian faith to any other beliefs, I acknowledge the need to examine black historical and cultural bearings to better equip black kingdomologists.

I agree with Timothy Bankole, who said,

> Putting Christ side by side with Buddha, Muhammad, or Confucius, I find a number of good and admirable attributes

74

in the religions of these leaders, but Christ to me stands out as unique. This is one reason why in spite of the many despicable and un-Christian acts committed by some Europeans in the name of Christianity, I have abandoned neither Christianity nor the Church. In my personal life, I have found Christ to be all-sufficient, and if Christianity is practiced as Christ taught it, I have no doubt whatever that God's kingdom will come and his will for mankind be accomplished even in our world and possibly in our time.[6]

As an African American, I was always interested in the truth about Africa and the relation of African religion to my own belief in Christianity. When I was twenty-six, I set out to learn about my heritage.

In Search of a Link

The prospect of discovering my link to African life was quite stimulating to me. I felt much as I had when I watched the last episode of *Roots*. Alex Haley had tracked his family tree all the way back to his clan, his tribe, and his history. It was exhilarating to watch the tears of excitement well up in his eyes. One could not help but share Haley's joy of knowing, "I have roots. I have a history. I have a link!"

When Europeans came to Africa, they did so with the idea that the African understood little, if anything, about God. They also had the idea that Africa had nothing to offer culturally or spiritually to the developing Western civilization. As we will observe shortly, this notion was false in the past and is equally false in the present. This ill-conceived notion is at the core of the contemporary misunderstanding of black people: our perspective, our methods, and our uniqueness. Furthermore, it is at the root of the misunderstanding of the black church.

In order to understand any of these matters, it is necessary to have a rendezvous with African Traditional Religion. This rendezvous provides the cultural antecedent for the development of the black church, black evangelicalism, and the subsequent impact and influence in America.

On a personal level, it helps me both to understand and to appreciate why the view of God held by my ancestors was so inclusive of all of life, resulting in the black church becoming central to black existence.

A major issue of debate among black historians and scholars is whether the slave adapted or lost his African religious heritage when he was brought to the Western hemisphere. The debate historically was waged between black historians W. E. B. DuBois[7] and E. Franklin Frazier.[8]

DuBois argued that the Negro church was the only institution among blacks that started in Africa and survived slavery. Contrary to DuBois, Frazier argued that it was impossible to establish any continuity between African religious practices and the Negro church in America. He argued that the crisis of slavery was too great to sustain African heritage. Moreover, the destruction of the native African languages marked the cessation of certain concepts that were incommunicable in English.

So then, the issue is whether blacks retained aspects of their African heritage. If we did not keep anything from Africa, then the African American experience is a totally new situation with no historical point of reference. However, if we did retain some aspects of our African heritage, we need to know what was salvaged for the sake of determining continuity between the continents.

The eminent black religious scholar Henry H. Mitchell convincingly argued in his book *Black Belief* that Dubois was right and Frazier was wrong. While not fully understood and appreciated today, much of what you see in contemporary black religion is not only what was seen in slavery, but also, to a large degree, what one saw in

Africa and, in fact, still sees in Africa. (I will discuss these similarities later in this chapter.)

Thus, to think of the black Christian church as merely a variant form of white missionary enterprise is fallacious. Rather, many of the fundamental viewpoints were already present; Europeans simply affixed Christian theology to an already existent theological and social structure.

My conviction is that the African heritage of the slave prepared him well for his encounter with the Bible. The tenets and theological structures of Christianity would not have been alien to him. In many cases, his own cultural and religious leanings would have helped him to theologize as efficiently as, and perhaps even more so than, his European counterpart.

The scenario is somewhat similar to that in Acts 17:22–24:

> So Paul stood in the midst of the Areopagus and said, "Men of Athens, I observe that you are very religious in all respects. For while I was passing through and examining the objects of your worship, I also found an altar with this inscription, 'To an Unknown God.' Therefore what you worship in ignorance, this I proclaim to you. The God who made the world and all things in it, since He is Lord of heaven and earth, does not dwell in temples made with hands."

Paul acknowledges the history of the Greeks' recognition of God by saying, "Some of your own poets have said, 'For we also are His children'" (v. 28). Paul was quoting the Cretan poet Epimenides (c. 600 BC).

As the apostle notes, the fact that we all stem from one seed certainly explains why certain patterns of belief in a supreme deity persist all over the globe. If a Greek could ascend to such grandiose thoughts of deity solely on the basis of general revelation, what would prevent the African from doing the same? The answer is nothing! All peoples grope for God. The difficulty is that our corrupt natures stifle our attempts to find an infinitely holy God. Mankind strains without efficacy through all sorts of ideological concoctions and images made by hand to reproduce the glory above.

Against this tendency to create a menagerie of pocket-sized deities made with hands, Paul is firm in condemning such practices in Acts 17:29. But we would be guilty of exegetical myopia if we did not recognize that Paul insinuates that Greeks may have had a profound understanding of the things above; yet this understanding was aberrant in places and was not effective toward salvation.

When one reads Aristotle's *Metaphysics*, one would think that Aristotle was a Christian. Many of Aristotle's postulations seem as though they were extracted from the Psalms. Perhaps this is why the Catholic theologian Thomas Aquinas found him so intriguing. It is clear in many respects that Aristotle was absolutely correct. But to my knowledge, no one ever confessed his sins and accepted Christ through reading the works of Aristotle.

My point is that if we listen carefully to the rhythmic cadence of African Traditional Religion, we will also find profound reflections of biblical truth that compel us to a greater appreciation for God, the Father of Jesus Christ, as well as for the Africans and their ability to remain committed to that God, even in the most oppressive circumstances.

In order to understand and appreciate the depth of the slaves' spiritual presuppositions, we must first grasp the process by which the African culture was transferred to America.

The Process of Cultural Transference

When people transfer or are transferred from one locale to another, they bring their culture with them, in varying degrees: their influences, habits, perspectives, dress, religious inclinations, and a myriad of other aspects of their past.

One has only to visit any major city in America to find a Chinatown, a little Italy, or a Germantown. Located in these specialized enclaves are specific things related to their particular histories and cultures. To dismantle these subcultures is no small feat. Why? In the same way that parents raise children with a view to influencing their future life orientation and decision-making, cultures also raise children so they have a distinct worldview that is hard to shake.

Because slavery was a nonvoluntary enterprise, the only hope the slave had to keep from becoming like his captor and losing his own self-identity in the process was remembering and reinforcing his own cultural heritage. Such was the case as slaves resisted attempts to be deculturalized.

When people take their cultures with them to a new locale, the central elements of the culture are the easiest to salvage, and the centerpiece of the West African culture was God. All of life was interpreted in terms of the Divine. Because God was the African slave's reference point for all of life, He would be the first one to whom the slave would appeal, particularly in a time of crisis.

The worldview of the majority of black Americans is the same as that of the captured African slave: God is central. This explains why the slave and their contemporary ancestors could not separate sacred from secular, personal sins from corporate sins, and religion from politics.

It is important to note here that low religious practices are a part of every religious environment. The Puritans conducted witch hunts to rid the colonies of witchcraft. Also, occultism existed among the peoples of Mesopotamia and in the worship of the mystery religions of the pre-Christian Hellenistic world. Therefore, African religion cannot be singled out as primitive savagery. As a matter of fact, there was no greater expression of low religion than the actions of American slave masters, who practiced inhumanity in the name of God.

But just as the low side of African religion survived in the Americas, so also did the high side. Because the high side was quick to acknowledge the Christian God, it was integrated into Christianity and sustained by it.

This cultural heritage was sustained through the process of reinforcement. This process of reinforcement made me reassess my criticism of the emotionalism of my ancestors in the black church, which evangelicals had taught me to reject as uninformed fanaticism.

This cultural transference was not lost during the trek of the Middle Passage, in which nearly twenty million Africans were made captive over the span of some three hundred years, 1517–1840. The slaves were continuously in touch with their African past because they were continuously in touch with each other. New slaves were constantly brought from Africa to the plantations, and they brought with them the African mindset, which served to reinforce the African disposition, even in the absence of tribal and language similarities. Segregation further fostered cultural continuation.

Another indication of cultural transference was the adoptive system the slave community developed. Coming from a tribal/clan background, the slave was dependent upon his communal environment for security, serenity, and society. The slave re-created that environment in establishing what E. Franklin Frazier, author of *The Negro Church in America*, called "the invisible institution." Christian clan meetings on the plantation became the new tribe. This is further verified in the slaves' migration from the South to the North. The plethora of "storefront" churches that arose in the North resulted from the slaves' demand for a tribal/clan concept to provide them with familiar surroundings in a hostile environment. Religion was the primary point of reference.

Understanding this concept helped me to make sense of the fact that anything significant, or even insignificant for that matter, happening in my community while growing up was either happening at the church, was sponsored by the church, or had to benefit the church. It also explains why the brightest and best black expertise and talent emerged out of the church.

A final method of cultural transference was the rise of the new African priest, the black preacher. The new Christianized leader of African people provided the cohesion and cultural reference point that kept the slaves in touch with the strengths of their past, the needs of their present, and the hopes for their future. Because African religion was handed down from one generation to the next by oral tradition, it would be natural for the African culture to continue to be transferred through that vehicle. The black preacher became the channel for this process. Black preachers were the new African point men in America who maintained the key elements of the African past.

Through an analysis of African Traditional Religion, we see that the African slave's capacity to understand Christian doctrine was not inhibited, but rather assisted, by his own cultural and religious predispositions. Furthermore, the liturgical basis for the slave church lay in these African traditions.

African Traditional Religion, although errant in many of its perspectives and applications—of utmost importance with regard to the understanding of the nature and identity of the one true God—contained a substantial foundation of similar systematic beliefs, thus allowing for the opportunity for a positive response to Christianity. Because it had such a high view of God, as well as a holistic view of spirituality, it made conversion to the biblical God and the mediator, Jesus Christ through the Holy Spirit, that much easier.

THE SIMILARITIES BETWEEN
AFRICAN RELIGION AND CHRISTIANITY

The slave was not a backward, savage person who had no perception of the true God. Yet, as can be said of all cultures, the African recognized God through "His invisible attributes" (Rom. 1:20) but not unto salvation, for salvation is through Jesus Christ. That mankind has a general consciousness toward God is a tenet of the first chapter of Romans. Yet, the gospel is the catalyst that affords all men salvation (vv. 16–17).

Since the slave trade primarily took its captives from West Africa, I begin our assessment of African heritage from that area. We will look at African Traditional Religion through the lens of a prominent group of West African people known as the Yoruba. For centuries, the Yoruba have lived in what today is western Nigeria. An examination of the Yoruba will provide us with a thorough and consistent view of the people of West Africa.

The Yoruba did not have a systematic, propositional theology as such; rather, theology was conveyed through the Odu, the vehicle of oral tradition. The Odu is a body of recitals used to convey the Yoruba doctrine and dogma.[9] There are some 256 of these Odu, and within them are 1,680 stories and myths, referred to as pathways, roads, and courses.[10] Some have verses that are almost unintelligible. Such sayings are supposed to be profoundly deep and require special knowledge to interpret. To remember all of this data was a gargantuan chore for the village storyteller, a feat far in excess of memorizing and reciting the entire King James Version of the Bible verbatim!

The question we face is, How did the African perceive his God? Often that perception was closer to Christianity than most Christians realize. There is a great deal of similarity between nine attributes of God as He is revealed in Scripture and that Supreme Being known to the Yoruba as Olodumare.

A Supreme Deity

As we observe the Yoruba form of African Traditional Religion, we see a very high view of the Supreme Deity known as Olodumare. For the Yoruba, the name Olodumare was magisterial and supreme beyond every other name. Does this sound familiar? Olodumare was preeminent over all, whether on the earth or in the heavens. All paid homage to him, including the pantheon of sub-deities (also referred to as the divinities) who owed their existence and allegiance to him. All acquiesced to his will without exception.[11]

This view of the supremacy of God was reiterated to me when I visited my grandmother. If a thunderstorm came through while I was at her home, she had me turn off the radio, the television, and all the lights, and sit quietly. Why? Because God was talking! She saw God as being in charge of all of life and as such, He demands our undivided attention.

For the Yoruba, theology was discourse about God, and it functioned within the matrix of life. Thoughts of Olodumare were always synthesized with the *Sitz im Leben* (situation in life) of the Yoruba. Yoruba theology was never an enterprise reduced to writing, because, like that of other tribes in Africa, it was passed down through oral recitation.

This "grapevine" approach to history and theology was and is a dominant part of black life. When my grandparents wanted to know what was happening in the community, the quickest and surest way to get that information was to go to the barbershop, the beauty shop, or the church house.

A God of Goodness and Justice

One of the fundamental characteristics of the African's God was His goodness and justice. There was no thought of God ever being unfair. One might think that the slave would have rejected his God because he was being enslaved in the name of God. Amazingly, he tenaciously clung to Him. The only rational reason for doing so would be that the slave's own understanding of God told him that his master's interpretation of God was incorrect.

One former missionary to Africa told me about a situation where a curse had been put on the animals in the community where the missionary lived. One after another for several days on end, animals were dying as had been forecast through the curse. Having had no previous exposure to spiritual warfare at this tangible a level, the missionary was disturbed by the reality of the situation to the point of exasperation. Seeing the frustration and hopelessness etched on the missionary's face, an African man with no formal education at all, yet with a faith in God intrinsic to his culture, asked the missionary in disbelief, "Je—hatahujui Mungu?" which translated means, "Do you even know God?"

The question was not intended as an insult, but rather as an honest desire to determine whether this missionary with years of biblical education who had supposedly "left all" to proclaim God in a foreign land even knew the God being proclaimed. The faith of the African man was firmly rooted in God, with or without any classroom education at all, but what he questioned was the faith of the missionary. Similarly, the faith of the African slave transported to America was firmly rooted in God, but what was questioned was the faith of the Christian whites claiming to know Him as well.

The slave's idea of God far exceeded that which was portrayed in the culture in which he lived, or he would never have loved, served, and worshiped the God of those who were enslaving, dehumanizing, and oppressing him. This fact alone demonstrates that African religion was not ignorant religion, but was socially applied religion. It related to the everyday realities of life. It did not rest solely on theological formulas but rather on the ethical realities of human existence. African religion addressed all of life: family life, community life, and business life. This explains why my ancestors looked to the church for direction in resisting the unjust system of American slavery.

This leads me to a major conclusion regarding God's twofold, sovereign purpose for American slavery. On one hand, slavery was allowed by God, not so much to teach the ignorant slave the right way, but rather, as in the case of Cornelius (Acts 10), to acknowledge the slave's faith in the true high God by introducing him to Jesus Christ, the Mediator who would replace all of the sub-deities as the means of access to God. On the other hand, I believe that slavery was allowed as the means by which God would introduce the true meaning of justice and spiritual liberation to American culture, which had neglected these aspects of His character.

The story of Joseph in Genesis 37–50 is an example. Joseph's final position was as second in command of all Egypt. However, his ascension to this lofty post was tortuous. Yet he told his brothers, "As for you, you meant evil against me, but God meant it for good in order to bring about this present result, to preserve many people alive" (Gen. 50:20).

This view affirms what America gained from this dreadful experience—a true vision of justice and spiritual freedom—and what slaves received—Jesus as their Savior and Mediator. If American society would submit to the justice of God the way slaves submitted to Jesus Christ as well as embrace the freedom given through a proper understanding of the cross and grace, then the power, presence, and impact of God in our culture would be beyond our wildest expectations.

A Creator God

Olodumare was the creator. In the genealogy of the gods, all other deities were created by Olodumare. All that existed owed its existence to him. Thus, the heavens and the earth were products of the creativity of Olodumare.

In much the same sense, Genesis 1:1 opens with an all-inclusive statement concerning the creativity of God (Elohim). Moses made use of a rhetorical device known as a *merism* ("the heavens and the earth") to demonstrate that Elohim created everything from the top, which is heaven, to the bottom, which is the earth, and all things in between.

Similar to the Hebrew tendency to use different names for God to emphasize different aspects of His character, Olodumare, in his capacity as creator, was known as Eleda. Also, because Olodumare was the origin and giver of life, he was called Elemi, "the Owner of the spirit" or "the Owner of life."

King of the Universe

Not only was Olodumare considered to be the creator, but he was "the king of the universe" as well. He was over humans and the other deities he created. We've already touched briefly on God's kingdom and His rule on earth, but other passages that delineate this aspect of God include Psalms 47, 93, and 96–99. These chapters are dedicated to the kingship of Yahweh. Psalm 93:1–2 reads, "The LORD [Yahweh] reigns, He is clothed with majesty; the LORD has clothed and girded Himself with strength; indeed, the world is firmly established, it will not be moved. Your throne is established from of old; You are from everlasting."

In much the same way that the Israelites used these "enthronement" psalms to acknowledge the majesty and authority of Yahweh, the Yoruba employed various chants that reflected the same ideas about Olodumare.

An Omnipotent God

To the Yoruba, Olodumare was also omnipotent. He was the most powerful being in the entire universe, able to do all things. The Yoruba would have had no difficulty at all grasping the truths in Genesis 18:14, Jeremiah 32:17, Matthew 19:26, and Luke 1:37, all of which affirm that there is nothing that God cannot do. The Yoruba thought also that things were possible only when and because they were ordered by Olodumare. Isaiah 46:9–10 affirms this same sentiment: that God orders all things after the counsel of His own will (see also Eph. 1:11). To put it simply, the black way of summarizing the great truth about God is to say, God can do anything except fail.

An Omniscient Deity

Olodumare was all-wise, all-knowing, and all-seeing. He and he alone was impeccable and omniscient. The sub-deities might err, but not the Supreme Deity. Olodumare was called Olorun when one referred to his wisdom. A line in one of the songs reads, *Kil'e nse ni bekulu t' oju olorun o to?*—"Whatever do you do in concealment that Olorun's eyes do not reach?"[12]

A similar analogy in Old Testament Scripture is found in Psalm 139. Yahweh is portrayed as the One who sees and knows all. Nothing is hidden from His sight. Or, as my grandmother would say, "Boy, God's a-watchin' you."

A Judge of All Things

E. Bolaji Idowu, author of *Olodumare God in Yoruba Belief,* says, "Olodumare is the final Disposer of all things. He is the Judge. He controls man's destiny, and each will receive from him as he deserves."[13]

This idea that God is the judge of the world is found in several places in Scripture. In Genesis 18:25, Abraham says that God is the "Judge of all the earth." Psalm 7:11 states that God is a "righteous judge." Romans 2:16 reports that one day God will judge men's secrets, while 1 Peter 4:5 says that He will "judge the living and the dead."

So strong was the appreciation for the sovereignty and justice of Olodumare that the Yoruba typically avoided seeking revenge for crimes perpetrated against them. They trusted that Olodumare would render proper recompense for evil. Wickedness would not receive

any impunity before Olodumare. "Vengeance is Mine, and retribu-
tion" (Deut. 32:35) would be totally in line with the Yoruba concept
of justice and sovereignty. In the mindset of the African and of his
progeny, the phrase *Fortune Imperatrix Mundi* (Fate, the ruler of the
world) never applied, for God was supreme, He ruled, and all would
answer to Him, without exception.

In America, we suffer from a "Rambo complex." We feel compelled to pay back evil for evil. If we do not pay back, we feel emas-
culated and spineless. It is much harder to let our need for revenge
go, knowing that God will always deal the last hand. Whereas this
concept of allowing God to judge is difficult for Americans, it has
always been a way of life for the Yoruba.

Far too often, we in the Western world tend to think that morality and impartiality are Western Christian concepts. Much to the
surprise of Western minds, this is not so. God's law is universal. The
morality is there because humans are image bearers. We need not try
to superimpose our cultural values upon people of diverse places, all
the while assuming that our cultural values are uniquely "Christian."
God has left a witness of Himself in all places.

An Immortal God

Immortality was foremost in the Yoruba concept of the Supreme
Deity. One Yoruba song states, "One never hears of the death of Olodumare." From excerpts of other Odu recitals, we find that Olodumare was known as the "Mighty, Immovable Rock that never dies."
As E. Bolaji Idowu comments, "In a sense, this is a comfort and
encouragement to the worshipping soul. It is necessary to know that
the Deity is alive forevermore, that He is unchanging in the midst of
all the changes and decay which have been the constant experience
of man, if religion and life are to have any ultimate meaning."[14] As in
Christianity, concomitant with the concept of immortality is that of
immutability (it follows from the infinite perfection of God that He

cannot be changed by anything from without Himself; and that He will not change from any principle within Himself).

A Sacrificial God

Sacrifice was an integral element of the life of the Yoruba. It was through the sacrificial system that one found approval before Olodumare and appeased the divinities. The basic idea was to seek favor from the gods and drive off the evil spirits.

Offerings were never offered directly to Olodumare, but through several mediators, some human (the priests) and some spiritual (the divinities). Only the divinities of the Yoruba bore the supplications of the people before the presence of the Supreme Deity. This was cosmic protocol. No one man could come near to Olodumare.

In Christianity, there is only one mediator between man and God (1 Tim. 2:5). Jesus alone is our advocate before the throne.

The Yoruba did at one time practice human sacrifice. Sometimes human sacrifices were offered so that they might be advocates before the divinities. Thus, the Africans would have had no problem whatsoever comprehending the role of Christ as sacrifice and advocate before the throne of God.[15]

Human sacrifice was often done in circumstances when the livelihood of the community was at stake. Usually, the victim was someone who had been captured in a war. Very seldom was the victim a member of the village; this happened only when a member of the tribe was slated to be an emissary for the community before the gods. Here again we see an advocate motif.

It is clear from the witness of Scripture that human sacrifice is an abominable practice, one that the Bible condemns. This was a detestable practice before God, and He made this known to Israel in Leviticus 20:1–2: "The LORD spoke to Moses, saying, 'You shall also say to the sons of Israel: "Any man from the sons of Israel or from the aliens sojourning in Israel who gives any of his offspring to

Molech, shall surely be put to death.""" All sacrifice was to be done after the prescription of God's edicts concerning sacrifice in Leviticus. This meant that there would be a categorical moratorium on human sacrifice of any kind!

Because the Yoruba had such a transcendent view of God, it was difficult for them to accept that the God of Christianity wanted to be near to them. Their concern was how a God so wonderful could come close to ones such as themselves. So then, the difficulty with the closeness of God as seen in the Bible was not born out of ignorance, but out of reverence. But as for the basic concept of mediation itself, the Yoruba had no problem, although certainly their views on the number of mediators required a significant alteration.

As we can clearly see, the Yoruba had an enormously deep appreciation for God and His ways. In fact, the appreciation was so profound that their belief system mirrored that of Christianity in many respects. Therefore, the leap from African Traditional Religion to Christianity would not have been a quantum leap, but rather a simple transition.

The discussion of similarities and disparities could go on *ad infinitum*, but it is sufficient to state that the African Traditional Religion of the Yoruba would have prepared them well for their entrée into Christianity. Also, from the heritage bestowed upon them by African Traditional Religion, three major repercussions entered into the African American church:

- the focus on oral communication
- the tendency toward orthodoxy and a supreme view of God
- an essential connection between theology and life

These three areas are at the heart of a comprehensive kingdom view of Christianity, and while the doctrine of God would not be articulated in terms of formal theological formulas in the African tradition, it would be communicated in the everyday interface of black life. My grandmother would formulate the doctrine simply: "He's so high you can't get over Him, He's so low you can't get under Him, He's so wide you can't get around Him." Somehow she found in this God from her African past all she needed to survive the cruel, harsh world of servitude and injustice.

Chapter 5

The Uniqueness of the Black Church

Today, in every major city in America, you can witness a growing number of African American churches that are offering comprehensive ministry to the whole of humanity without compromising the Word of God. These individuals and ministries are committed to biblical preaching, lifestyle accountability, and personal evangelism, but have rejected the social secularism and eschatological escapism of much of the contemporary evangelical church. They are intentionally building communities. As a result, people's lives are being improved by things such as job skill and placement programs, mentors for the fatherless, business development, GED programs, and a myriad of other life-enhancing outreaches.

This contemporary movement is helping with the historical black church's fusion of the best of African culture and the Christian faith. Such a fusion gives rise to what is probably one of the clearest expressions of New Testament Christianity America has ever seen. This is so because of the natural way the slave community accepted Christianity, coupled with the similarities that existed between the experience of the Jews in both the Old and New Testaments. Such a link made untenable any philosophical separation of church and state, for one could not speak of life apart from theology.

When we examine the New Testament definition of the church and juxtapose it with the functioning of the historical black church, it becomes clear that the two institutions were very similar. As such, these two institutions are in a unique position to teach both the black and white churches of today what true biblical Christianity looks like when it operates in a church that truly makes God the center of its existence.

THE BIRTH OF THE AFRICAN AMERICAN CHURCH

It is unfortunate that many people see the origin of the African American church as little more than a branch that emerged from mainstream white Christianity. When one comes to understand and appreciate fully the circumstances that came together to give rise to this unique institution, it becomes clear that its makeup consisted of men and women of tremendous depth, intellect, wisdom, and pride who were willing to submit all of these virtues to the work of a sovereign God. There is no understanding or appreciation of the black experience without understanding the importance and centrality of the black church.

The birth of the African American church was the result of a confluence of five strategic factors: the slaves' search for meaning, evangelization, a natural integration of their religious foundations, the Bible, and the black preacher.

The Slaves' Search for Meaning

The reality of slavery forced the slave to look for meaning. Slaves found themselves in a precarious position: they had no freedom, no meaning, no hope, and no help. Where then were they to turn to find these desperately needed facets of life? They looked to the only

94

place available, which was within their history, their culture, and their religious heritage. There they saw the most significant aspect of their past life in Africa: God!

In his book *Black Belief,* Henry Mitchell said, "It is probable that this African, holistic praise of God was also such an important affirmation of Black selfhood that its sense of 'God all in me' was among the most important resources for survival in the unprecedented dehumanization of American slavery."[1] They had to look to that God whom they celebrated in West Africa for His provision of meaning, hope, and freedom, to give them that same definition of existence in their new hostile environment. Immediately, the slaves had the one thing that could keep them keeping on despite the social reality of their plight—they had their God.

Thus, the slaves' minds were already preconditioned for the key role the black church would play in their lives. This intuitive theistic mindset also reveals the depth of the divine consciousness within them.

Evangelization

White organizations, such as the Anglican Society for the Propagation of the Gospel, and movements such as the first Great Awakening, began evangelizing the slaves.[2] What is critical to understand here is that this evangelization process occurred without addressing the slaves' oppressed condition. In 1667, for example, the Virginia legislature agreed that baptism did not alter the state of the slave. Such laws allowed blacks to be evangelized without those evangelizing them ever having to address their sociopolitical plight.

With the influence of the first Great Awakening, Christianity was brought to the level of the common man. This made the African feel comfortable with the appeal of Christianity, especially since the slave was as common a man as you could find. Many of these revivals and crusade meetings were full of emotion, shouting, dancing, and other physical and verbal expressions. This reminded the slaves of their own worship experiences and helped to make the structure of American Christianity palatable to them.

A Natural Integration of Their Beliefs

Slaves began integrating their African beliefs with the new Christian revelations. When they heard the message of the gospel, they heard more than just personal forgiveness of sin. They heard the voice of hope. The Christian message spoke of heaven where earthly trials would be no more and where they would find freedom from all the injustices they were experiencing. They heard about a God who loved them and suffered for them so that they might experience eternal freedom. Given the cry for freedom and the magnitude of God's suffering love, with which the slave could easily identify, the stage was set for finding that freedom in Christ.

In Christianity the slaves also found a message of liberation from the oppressive historical condition of slavery. They latched on to the Christian message as their means for survival, self-authentication, and historical freedom.

The integration of the eternal and the temporal was evidenced in the worship services of the slaves. They would dress up for their worship services and mimic some of their African rituals in this new Christian environment. They held secret worship meetings if the master did not officially allow them to gather together because he rejected the Christianization of the slave or he feared possible insurrection. At these secret meetings the slaves developed codes to communicate with each other. They communicated these codes in slave songs.[3] This was a major means of communication in the African Traditional Religion. For example, one of the slaves would start singing, "Steal away, steal away to Jesus." Translation: "When the sun goes down there will be a church meeting in the swamp, so steal away to the service."

Songs, then, were not just for personal pleasure. They were also a mechanism for community planning, again revealing the strong intellectual and organizational prowess of the slaves as well as their willingness to risk punishment in order to maintain their worship of the supreme God.

Swamps and forests became the early sanctuaries for slave services. On the morning after a worship service, the slaves in the field would break out with a song, "I couldn't hear nobody praying." Translation: "The master did not hear our worship service going on."

The early African slave church, then, was made up of a brilliant cadre of men and women who had to encode their communication in the natural movement of their lives, with God at the center.

The Bible

The Bible became the first book to which the slaves were exposed. They became acutely aware that the Bible was deeply concerned with the subject of freedom in history as well as in eternity. God had worked in the past with another group of people called the Israelites, who were, like the Africans, under bondage in a foreign land.

As the story unfolded, it became clear that God was not only concerned about their condition because of His love for them, but He also desired to release them from bondage so that they could worship Him freely. The slaves concluded that if God could save Israel from Egyptian oppression, He could certainly save black people in America. Thus the biblical story of Israel's deliverance was a story that was easy for the slaves to transpose to their own experience. It became clear that God was on the side of the slaves and against the oppression of their masters. Israel's story became the black community's "story."[4] This also gave the slave a more comprehensive understanding and approach to the Bible than their white counterparts possessed.

The Black Preacher

The fifth and final factor that led to the development of the black church was the rise of the black preacher, who would provide the link between Africa and America. We will look at this unique leader in the next chapter.

THE AFRICAN AMERICAN CHURCH AND CHRIST

The African American church did not arrive at its Christology through academic study, but rather through the context of slavery. This is not to say that academic information was not available to the black church, but rather that the black church was forced to answer specific questions that reflected the journey from slavery to freedom.

For example, the slaves sang,

> *I want Jesus to walk with me,*
> *I want Jesus to walk with me,*
> *All along my pilgrim's journey*
> *I want Jesus to walk with me.*
> *In my trials, walk with me,*
> *In my trials, walk with me,*
> *When the shades of life are falling,*
> *Lord, I want Jesus to walk with me.*
> *He walked with my mother; He'll walk with me.*
> *He walked with my mother; He'll walk with me.*
> *All along my pilgrim's journey*
> *I know Jesus will walk with me.*

The slaves saw Jesus as a present reality, providing the impetus, support, and direction for their journey. The experience of slavery never allowed the black church to get caught up in the theological and philosophical meaning of Jesus, because the Jesus in black religion was a practical deliverer of the oppressed. Neither, however, did they allow this temporal emphasis to decrease their appreciation of the deity of Christ.

Whereas white preachers and theologians often defined Jesus Christ as a spiritual Savior, the Deliverer of people from personal sin and guilt, African American preachers viewed God as the Liberator in history. The black church saw in Jesus One who suffered as they were suffering; One who had experienced oppression as they were experiencing oppression. Yet, they also saw One who was able, by virtue of His divine power, to overcome the chains of enslavement. The acts and deeds of Jesus' life and ministry were literal acts and deeds, designed to provoke trust and commitment in the midst of present calamity, as the slave songs clearly demonstrated. A similar example can be seen in Thomas A. Dorsey's song "This Man Jesus":

> *Jesus walked the water and so raised the dead*
> *He made the meats for those saints   He multiplied the bread*
> *The blinded eyes He opened and cleansed the lepers too.*
> *Then died to save sinners—Now what more could Jesus do?*
> *This man never will leave you—This man will not deceive you.*
> *This man waits to relieve you—when troubles are bearing you*
>   *down.*
> *Oh, this man when danger is near you—This man is ready*
>   *to cheer you.*
> *This man will always be near you—He is a wonderful Savior*
>   *I've found.*[5]

This song shows Jesus as actually involved in the liberation process in His earthly life—"blinded eyes He opened"—as well as transcending what occurs now for those who know Him. This illustrates how the "was-ness" and "is-ness" of Jesus are wedded in the black religious experience.

Harold Carter argues in his book *The Prayer Tradition of Black People* that the New Testament provided the slave community with a Christ with whom they could identify. He says, "The slave found in the person of Jesus, a savior, a friend, and fellow sufferer at the hands of unjust oppressor, who would do anything but fail."[6] Carter continues, "Doctrines about his theological nature were subordinate to this pragmatic power in life. He was experienced as a savior and a friend. There was no human condition that Jesus could not meet."[7]

At this point, you might again question how the slaves became so amenable to the Savior of those who used Him to enhance black enslavement. The answer is found in the slaves' African past.

In the African religion, God was so high that it took a plethora of mediators to help people reach God. Thus, virtually everything, both inanimate and animate, was called upon to help the African reach the most high God, and he still fell short. When the slaves were confronted with the Mediator, Jesus Christ, however, they found in Him the solution to their greatest religious problem. With Christ, no other mediator was needed to get to God.

Because Christ was the God-man, the slaves not only solved their divine problem—namely, access to the high God—but they also solved a very historical problem. Perfect humanity provided the slaves with someone who could liberate them in history from any and every kind of problem, injustice, and oppression. Sadly enough, this aspect of Christ's work was ignored and misunderstood by the broader Christian society.

Carter agrees that traditional religion from West Africa gave blacks an orientation that allowed them to adapt easily to Jesus:

It was not hard for Black people to assign to Jesus literal powers. He "came in my sick room." He "cooled scorching fever and calmed troubled minds." He was a "heart fixer and mind regulator." He was a "lawyer in the courtroom, doctor in the sick room, friend to the friendless, husband to the widow, mother to the motherless, and father to the fatherless." He saved from sin, had power over the "devil," and guided his children with his eye. All these basic deeds were continually attributed to him in prayer.[8]

The reason that prayer could be made to Jesus in this manner is because His earthly life and ministry demonstrated that He cared and had the power to make a difference. The slaves found a biblical liberation in the Scripture. The African American church saw the liberation motif of the Old Testament and the teaching of the New Testament, combined with the reality of the black religious experience, as validating the existence of Christ as Savior from personal sin as well as Deliverer of the oppressed.

From a biblical perspective, the natural questions here are whether human liberation can be demonstrated to be part and parcel of Jesus' ministry and whether He can be demonstrated to be the very ground of human liberation, as black religion asserts. The answer is an unqualified *yes* on both counts. The black church was on strong theological footing in seeing Christ as the basis for liberation from oppression. Although such recognition was not understood in exegetical formulas, it was nonetheless biblically sound and the clearest and earliest expression of this Christological theme in America.

The white church needs this Christological understanding if oneness is to be achieved. On the other hand, the contemporary African American church must make sure it does not lose its historically strong spiritual foundation as we seek to expand our social influence and impact. We must not be like Israel, which was an oppressed community in the New Testament because it was in bondage to Rome. Their Christology took them to the point where they recognized Jesus as the One with the message of the kingdom and the power to miraculously relieve their condition of oppression. Yet, when they sought to make Him an earthly king (John 6:15), He refused.

The problem was that a Christology that only leads to political, social, and economic reform is insufficient. Human liberation is part of a comprehensive kingdom agenda theology predicated on spiritual salvation. This is why Jesus said, "Repent, for the kingdom of heaven is at hand" (Matt. 4:17) and why He told Nicodemus, "Unless one is born again he cannot see the kingdom of God" (John 3:3).

Human liberation is also predicated on a willingness to obey Christ as Master. Thus, the process of liberation must be willing to incorporate the principles of Christ if it would present Christ as the leader of the struggle. This is why Jesus said to His followers, "Why do you call Me, 'Lord, Lord,' and do not do what I say?" (Luke 6:46).

Applying this to the black experience means that it is improper Christology to say that Christ is leading the struggle against American racism if He is not first enthroned in the lives of those involved in leading the liberation. The fact that liberation is taking place under the banner of Jesus Christ is not a sufficient statement in and of itself. The leadership must possess both a proper saving relationship to Christ and a proper biblical methodology before the black church can ever return to the strength it has experienced in the past.

The Communal Nature of the Black Church

The historical black church also reminded the slave of who he was in the sight of God, rather than man. One who was considered a "boy" on the plantation became Deacon Jones on Sunday. An elderly woman who was known as a "girl" during the week by her mistress became Mother Smith on Sunday. The church was crucial for maintaining God's view of black dignity and significance under the hand of a good God.

The black church viewed itself as more than just a loose gathering of individuals. It saw itself as a community in which everyone was related. This communal mindset again owed its existence to the African worldview. In Africa, tribal life was family life, and family life was also religious life. E. Bolaji Idowu describes this interrelationship:

The household grew into the compound—which is usually an oblong or circular enclosure of houses with a common space in the middle and made up in the main of the family which has been extended through procreation, through the living together of blood relations, and the addition to them of "strangers" who came or were brought to dwell among them. In such a compound, there is the central house, a shrine which is dedicated to the common ancestor. Worship here is undertaken by the supreme head of the extended family who is "father" or "grandfather" to the whole community. The whole community is the offspring of the ancestor as well as of the central tutelary divinity. This supreme head is entitled to his priestly function because he is the senior of the blood relations in the extended family and therefore succeeds to the priestly function which used to belong to the common ancestor from whom the family descended.[9]

Within the tribal clan, people found support, affirmation, value, protection, meaning, purpose, and guidance. All of these things were experienced in a context of love—with God at the center of tribal life.

When the slaves came to America, the new tribe, of which God was the center, was the black church. Rather than accepting the broader society's definition of church, which oftentimes lacked communal life, they reached back to their African understanding of family. This communal perspective was reflected in the way people related to each other as uncle, aunt, cousin, brother, or sister. This perspective was also responsible for the black church being a successful, beneficial brotherhood that took care of its sick, supported its widows and orphans, educated its children, and developed its independent financial base.

The parallel between the image of the church in Scripture and the communal emphasis of the black church is obvious. The church is to be viewed as a community, that is, a group of individuals inseparably linked together. In the New Testament the church is referred to as the household of the faith (Gal. 6:10), God's household (Eph. 2:19; 1 Peter 4:17), and a spiritual house (1 Peter 2:5). Christians viewed fellow Christians as fellow citizens (Eph. 2:19) and members of one another (Rom. 12:5; Eph. 4:25).

The church is further seen as a tightly knit community by the emphasis on its oneness. Although it is made up of many members, it is one body (1 Cor. 12:20) that suffers together (1 Cor. 12:26) and is fitted and held together (Eph. 4:16). Because all of its spiritual gifts come from one Lord, there is to be no schism in the one body (1 Cor. 12:3–5, 25–31). This mandate for oneness extends beyond the confines of the black church to include the body of Christ at large.

A Natural Ministry to the Poor

Internally, the first church began selling "their property and possessions and were sharing them with all, as anyone might have need" (Acts 2:45). This was a voluntary act, not a governmentally imposed social system, of meeting each other's needs so that there would be no unnecessary physical suffering. While the New Testament does not make it imperative that the church use the same exact method of sharing, the church is obligated to meet the physical needs of its members.

The church is commanded to provide money for poor believers' food (Acts 11:28–30; Rom. 15:25–27; 2 Cor. 8:3–4), clothing (James 2:15), and the world's goods in general (1 John 3:17). This can be done by individual members (James 2:15–16) and by the church corporately (2 Cor. 8:18–22). People who are to benefit from the church's internal outreach are those who have suffered misfortune, such as the widows who have no foreseeable means of support (1 Tim. 5:9–10), orphans (James 1:27), and the poor (1 John 3:17).

Because God gives the earthly poor great spiritual riches—namely, faith and future reward—it is an insult to God's value system to treat the poor in an inferior way. The apostle James called the early church to accountability in this area (James 2:5).

James refers to the rich Christians who are dishonoring the poor as "beloved brethren." This does not excuse their acts, but only shows that James saw that their sin of oppression had nothing to do with their salvation, which was a gift from God. They were at the same time brethren and "judges with evil thoughts" (James 2:4 NIV). Here we see that oppression is nothing new to the church, but that such activity is condemned by God and should be vigorously resisted.

The church also has a social responsibility to the broader non-Christian society: "Then, while we have opportunity, let us do good to all people, and especially to those who are of the household of the faith" (Gal. 6:10). It is the responsibility of the church to "speak the truth" about the sin of oppression to the whole culture.

After Peter and the other apostles were freed from prison, they spoke about Jesus in the temple, a direct violation of the Sanhedrin's command for them not to teach others about Christ. When they were arrested again and brought before the council, Peter justified their violation by saying, "We must obey God rather than men" (Acts 5:29). This shows us that whenever a religious or civil ruling body (the Sanhedrin had both religious power and wide political power[10]) contradicts what God has said or commanded, we are justified to disobey its laws.

God commanded the church to be equitable and honest in its dealings with the unbelievers (1 Peter 2:12), to work honest labor to sustain oneself and family (1 Tim. 5:8), to be hospitable to strangers (Heb. 13:2), to practice justice and fairness (Col. 4:1), and to hold no social distinctions (James 2:1). Therefore, if society (or religion or government) thwarts our efforts to obey these commands, the church has a basis for godly, biblically based rebellion.

In addition, when the government fails to fulfill its divine responsibility of promoting justice (Rom. 13:1–5), then Christians have the right and responsibility to resist, as long as such resistance is within Christian behavior. Paul exhibited an act of civil disobedience; he refused to obey the command of the chief magistrates of Philippi when they asked him to leave jail after he had been illegally beaten.[11] Such an act was justified, however, because the civil authority was unjust. Paul "was trying by legitimate means to compel the Roman authorities to fulfill their God-appointed task. It is to be noted that he did not stage his sit-in because of some selfish personal claim against the authorities."[12]

The black church and the civil rights movement that it spawned, then, stands on solid biblical ground as a liberating community. However, that ground is only as solid as its biblical moorings. A task of black kingdomologists in the contemporary black church is to continue to direct and keep its teachings in tune with biblical methodology. A conspicuous absence of correct theology leads to a number of weaknesses that can plague a society, as is evidenced in the resultant effect of the embracing of a victim mentality. Applying a biblical understanding to struggles within the culture is the only example of authentic solutions that ought to be presented to the broader society on how to address social issues through the private sector.

This biblical approach should apply to all of the problems our society faces today, including housing, employment, education, and poverty. The historical black church, with little or no governmental support, was the spiritual hub that connected the community spokes of black-owned and operated businesses, the black press, black colleges, and community-based mutual aid societies.

The black church has deposited in its biblical legacy and cultural history the clearest model of biblical Christianity in the history of American religion. This is not because the black church is innately superior to the white church, but because it historically operated more in line with the comprehensive nature of biblical revelation and a kingdom orientation. It did so because the communities' cultural-historical roots and worldview, coupled with the reality of American slavery and racism, forced the black church to grapple with aspects of biblical revelation that were unnecessary for the majority culture to have to deal with in any comprehensive manner.

The contemporary black kingdomologist church stands on a unique pinnacle to be the visual form of the assets of incarnational Christianity: that is, Christianity that visibly displays itself in culture-wide influence, lifestyle, and social ethics. Such assets also include corporate compassion, comprehensive biblical justice, the celebrative nature of worship, holistic ministry, and an integration between the social and the spiritual.

Far from being an uneducated, erratic, and inept folk religion, the historical black church in America was the primary proving ground for biblical Christianity. It uniquely demonstrated the relationship between love and justice. It demonstrated the nature of the church as a family and community of believers rather than simply a gathering of individualized family units. The black church personified the relationship between faith and works and how that relationship transcends the personal matters of life and enters into the spheres of politics, economics, social justice, and law.

The great mosaic of the historical black church shows that there was no distinction between secular and sacred. The church demonstrated clearly that the purpose of the sacred is that it might invade the secular and transform it. It reflected and transmitted God as the epicenter of life, all of life, and it demanded that culture be called to task for any failure to recognize Him as such.

If the lessons of the historical black church are instructional for the culture at large, then they are even more so for the black community itself. If the historic black church, using biblical principles, was able to solidify us, sustain us, protect us, promote us, house us, clothe us, feed us, employ us, and represent us during the worst of times, then how much more should we now appeal to that same biblically based authority today. The black church no longer needs artificial motivators to give us dignity. With God, our African heritage, and our black church experience we already have all we need to humbly stand tall. In God's definition of us, we operate in a secure identity because who we are is rooted in a sovereign, immutable Being who has the last word about all things.

Challenges for uniting today in the black church do exist, and I would be remiss not to mention them. They revolve around the contemporary presence of diversity that has arisen within the black church due to the changes in the economic status of our constituencies, increased mobility, the influence of social media, and our functioning in more integrated communities. We also face the current development of internal class divisions, which present an obstacle concerning how to stay connected as a unified whole and maintain the solidarity that is a necessary component to having any lasting impact on improving the status of urban America. The current increase in the number of megachurches operating with multi-staffed ministries has produced, to some degree as well, a disconnect from the traditional "storefront" churches still in existence. Despite our many differences, though, our singleness of focus must revolve around Jesus Christ and the sensitivity He has shown to social justice and racism, even though our approach may vary greatly as to how to enact solutions.

Not only do we as the black church need to unite together in order to address the many issues plaguing our society, but we also must join hands with our white brothers and sisters, inviting them to work alongside us to impact change within the current dysfunctional trends in our community and in theirs.

The Bible stands as the only sufficient authority and source for providing the appropriate basis for the role of the church in society. Only by allowing the Bible, operating through committed Christians in both the black and white church, to be the standard by which we judge ourselves and others, can we reexperience the power necessary to be the kind of salt and light that can save a decaying society.

The church must operate across racial lines, recognizing and using every legitimate avenue to change every expression or repercussion of racism, classism, sexism, and separatism, as well as all other forms of social unrighteousness. Yet, we in the black church must never allow their existence to so cripple us that we are immobilized. A generation of children simply cannot wait until other people change things for us.

It is time once again for the church to *be* the church.

Chapter 6

The Role of
the Black Preacher

Without question, the black preacher in America has been the
most visible, vocal, influential, and strategic leader black
America has ever had. On both a personal and corporate level, he has
been used to bring hope, direction, encouragement, and deliverance
to a people needing all of the above.

Personally, I have had the unique blessing of having been influenced and encouraged by many godly and effective preachers and
pastors. One such person is the Rev. Charles Brisco, the former pastor
of the Paseo Baptist Church in Kansas City, Missouri. He epitomizes
the historical significance and greatness of the black preacher to the
black church and black community. As spiritual leader he faithfully
taught his people God's Word. As community leader he served on the
Kansas City school board and helped shape the school system into
one of excellence and justice.

I have observed with great admiration his loving, tender care for
his congregation in the way he greeted them, cared for them when
they were sick, and corrected them when they needed it. One of his
members summed him up endearingly when she said, "Our pastor

loves us." I've also admired Pastor Brisco's commitment to his family. Whatever progress I have made as a pastor I owe in part to his influence in my life. Of profound impact was his statement to me early on in my ministry that encouraged me to remember that our people in the black community needed to be challenged at another level theologically but that delivering that challenge, even if it was critical at times, had to be done out of a heart of love and not merely as a critique or correction.

The late Tom Skinner is another black evangelical preacher who had a significant impact in shaping my preaching both in style and content. Tom entered my life as a mentor, and later became a dear friend. I was captivated early on, like everyone else, by Tom's fiery oratory, his biblical commitment, and his contemporary relevance. His preaching mesmerized black and white listeners alike with his passionately delivered evangelistic message rooted in a kingdom emphasis.

Tom Skinner possessed a courage far exceeding most, and he challenged the white establishment theologically on social issues at a time when it was grossly unpopular to do so. And yet, his commitment to a thoroughly biblical worldview led him to also challenge the black church in areas where it needed improvement as well. Tom was ahead of his time socially and theologically, and because of his presence the road was paved for people like me. He personally encouraged me in my academic pursuits because he recognized the great need for black evangelicals to be able to sit at the academic table of discussion alongside white brothers and sisters to offer a perspective on the Bible and theology that reflected the black experience and interpreted social justice through a biblical lens. Tom wanted me, and others like me, to gain access to the tools of theology that white theologians possessed in order to use them in a way, and on subject matters, that they had not previously been applied.

Dr. A. L. Patterson, one of the all-time leading black preachers in America, also left his mark on me in many ways. In my fiery desire to bring a strong biblically based message to the black community, Dr. Patterson personally exhorted me to never lose sight of my connection to the community I hoped to reach. He challenged me to always stay in touch through authentic relationships in order to best affirm the strengths within the black community by having seen them up close on a daily basis rather than resort to merely critiquing theological aspects that needed to be improved.

Dr. John McNeal, founder and senior pastor of Atlanta Bible Baptist Church as well as a former dean of students and professor at Carver Bible College, invested in my life as well outside of the classroom by pouring into me the conviction to not just preach the Word, but to live up to the Word that is preached.

What is the history of these godly men, and others, to whom the whole black community owes a huge debt of gratitude for their leading us from oppression to freedom? As with the black church, we will find that the roots of the black preacher lie in the African Traditional Religion.

THE EMERGENCE OF THE BLACK PREACHER

The priest in the African Traditional Religion was characterized by his ability to remember the proverbs and stories (Odu) and communicate them to the members of the tribal communities in an accurate and effective manner. He provided a link between their past and their present. The priest, then, was the embodiment of the history, culture, and heritage of the tribe. H. Beecher Hicks describes this role in his book *Images of the Black Preacher*:

> The vast power of the priest in the African state is well known; his realm alone—the province of religion and medicine—remained largely unaffected by the plantation system. The Negro priest, therefore, early became an important figure

113

on the plantation and found his function as the interpreter of the supernatural, the comforter of the sorrowing, and as the one who expressed, rudely but picturesquely, the longing and disappointment and resentment of a stolen people.[1]

It is little wonder that the black preacher has perpetually served as a father figure to black people, seeing to their welfare in all spheres of life, whether social, political, economic, or spiritual.

The Black Preacher as Father Figure

The New Testament church leaders had little trouble viewing their followers from a paternal perspective. Thus, Paul could call Timothy his son (2 Tim. 1:2) and Titus his child (Titus 1:4). John could call Christians he was teaching his children (1 John 2:1, 12) and even explain their varying spiritual status within the framework of the different levels of family structure: namely, fathers, young men, and children (1 John 2:13–14). Thus, it is normal to hear black pastors refer to the preachers they ordain as their sons in the ministry.

Here again the African past prepared the preacher well for his posture within the Christian church. While this parental role has at times been abused by some black preachers, it has also served as the driving force behind the development and survival of the black church, in much the same way that the apostle Paul's loving yet firm parental role directed the church at Thessalonica (1 Thess. 2:7–12).

The Black Preacher as Priest

The African priestly heritage explains the posture of the preacher as spiritual representative of black people before God. Because God is viewed as a comprehensive part of all of life, the black preacher has traditionally represented God's presence and leadership in every part of black life.

Because God is the center of all of life, Sunday morning involves every aspect of the community. Announcements, for instance, have a dominant place in black services. This announcement period facilitates the wedding between the priest, oral tradition, community life, and the centrality of God. The service gave the preacher a weekly platform with which to guide his people in the comprehensive application of faith to life.

The presence of the priest also provided cohesiveness for the tribe or clan. He served as the point person for their relationship with one another as well as their individual and collective relationship with God. He led them in their ceremonies and festivals, which reflected the essence of tribal life, and he served as the foundation and leader for the totality of the life, activities, and perspectives of the whole community.

Black churches became the new clans, and the black preacher was the new priest. Because access to the formal religious structures of the broader society (white denominations and educational institutions) was virtually nonexistent, black preachers were relatively free to draw intuitively on their African past for many of the elements that would become aspects of black worship. Henry Mitchell says in *Black Preaching*:

> The preaching tradition of the Black ancestors did not spring into existence suddenly. It was developed during a long and often quite disconnected series of contacts between the Christian gospel, variously interpreted, and African men and women caught up in the Black experience of slavery and oppression. To this experience and this gospel they brought their own culture and folkways. In a manner more unusual and powerful than they or we dreamed—until recent decades—they devised a Black preaching tradition. This preaching tradition consisted of the ways Blacks delivered and responded to sermons.[2]

As the African Traditional Religion required the presence of the priest to link the people to each other and to God, the various small gatherings that were part of the black church required the presence of a Christian pastor. Therefore, as these new clan gatherings developed, the roles of the African priest and the Christian pastor merged within the black preacher. The white community allowed the black preacher to have this power, because the position of a pastor who was responsible for providing spiritual leadership to local congregations was within the broader Christian structure.

The African American preacher had significant contact with Anglos and, therefore, was in the unique position to learn, analyze, and interpret their ways. His knowledge had to be communicated to the slave community in such a way as to simultaneously teach the slave about God, protect the slave against oppression, lead the community into a dualistic understanding of freedom (temporal and eternal), and stay within the framework of the social and religious boundaries of the slave master. It should be obvious why it was often the most skilled and intuitive who rose to the position of black preacher.

Neither the slave preacher nor the developing black church was hampered in the pursuit of the God of justice because of limited access to academic training. Theology was transmitted orally, from preacher to preacher. This is the only way to explain the perpetual dissemination of the great Christian themes despite the denial of even an elementary level of education.

The Bible became the authoritative sourcebook for the preacher and his congregation's developing understanding of God. However, the Bible was not used as a means of developing an esoteric epistemology. When the black preacher opened his Bible, it was more for the interpretation of recent experience than for detailed exegetical analysis. The different preaching styles between the black and white preacher resulted from their different goals: the black preacher looked to the Bible for an ethical view of life that met the personal needs of the members of his community; the white preacher looked for an epistemological system of thought.

The black preacher, rather than being inferior, had an exceptional ability to lead, communicate, memorize, interpret the times, and link the past with the present. To think that he was able to do this with little or no formal education, opposition from the broader culture, and barely any money is nothing short of miraculous. This fact should dispel any notion of black inferiority and, to the contrary, is an argument for the scholarship of black preachers in the realm of applied theology.

THE LEADERSHIP OF
THE AFRICAN AMERICAN PREACHER

As I mentioned earlier, the African slave saw himself in the saga of the Jewish people, as told from Exodus through the book of Joshua. Moreover, deep in the recesses of his heart he knew that the God who broke the yoke of slavery for Israel could do the same for him. Thus, the slave structured his mental and spiritual framework to complement that of ancient Israel.

Just as the dilemma of Israel required Moses and Joshua to be great spiritual, political, and military leaders, so it was in the African American community. This perspective produced leaders from Richard Allen[3] to Martin Luther King Jr. The holocaust of slavery originally forged this union of priest and presiding officer, and the continued oppression continued the need for the man of God to lead the way.

"The black preacher has been called upon by politicians, parishioners, peacemakers and all others," said black historian Charles V. Hamilton. "He has been a natural leader in the black community. He has a fixed base, the church; he has a perpetual constituency, the congregation, which he sees assembled for at least one to two hours each week . . . then the preacher's contact far exceeds one or two hours."[4]

The key word that summarizes the leadership role of the black preacher is *link*. He has the perpetual responsibility of tying together the old and the new. This is clearly demonstrated on the four cataclysmic fronts of the cultural transformations black people have experienced:[5]

- the transition from African freedom to American slavery;
- the transition from American slavery to American freedom during Reconstruction;
- the transition from the South to the North during and following World War I;
- the transition from segregation to integration during the civil rights movement.

This leadership role is sometimes perceived as inferior because it focuses on the social and political aspects of life in addition to the theological and spiritual. Such a position, however, results from limited criteria. There were aspects that were inferior, not because they were social or political, but because the method used did not always reflect biblical methodology. Similarly, white preachers who vehemently "contended for the faith" in their legitimate war against the onslaught of liberalism during the early part of the twentieth century did not reflect biblical methodology. Despite their academic knowledge of the Bible, it did not reflect itself in practical social terms. Thus they could argue for the virgin birth while simultaneously maintaining racism, segregation, and classism. Their methodology then operated in a very limited sphere and fell far short of biblical requirements or expectations.

The problem in both cases is a failure to be thoroughly biblical, for God has given a kingdom agenda—clear theological guidelines to govern the social, spiritual, and political issues of life.[6] Anglo Christians did not understand that African American preachers were simply bringing another issue to the theological table that needed to be "contended with," and therefore, their work was written off as social, not spiritual, and by definition inferior.

Yet the issues of slavery and inference were not merely matters of politics and states' rights. They were matters of what was right before God. There was nothing Christian about the dehumanization of one person by another. Where the Bible says, "Love your neighbor as yourself" (James 2:8), it does not mince words. There is nothing neighborly about subjecting a person to something that strips that person of dignity, freedom, and hope since all mankind is created in the image of God (Gen. 1:26–28).

Furthermore, where the Bible is a strong advocate of the family and fidelity in marriage, slave owners used sexual relations (which God had given mankind to make more image bearers) as a tool for breeding "stock," as though the slave owners were trying to produce the next Derby winner.

The very institution of slavery in America was unbiblical since it was predicated on kidnapping, which was a capital crime (Ex. 21:16). It was imperative that the black preacher voice his concerns as a political activist—but, more important, as a man of God—on this theological issue. For such was the role of a prophet.

Although blacks were no longer wearing iron shackles after the Civil War, other shackles were still there. The new shackles were now set in writing: "Whites Only" or "Colored Restrooms Here." The "master" had also changed. He now wore a suit, and the whip was his ability to deny access to opportunity and equality. Just as the early slave preachers were to lead their people to freedom, even so the task of the preacher remains the same in contemporary America.

Such a consistent posture is not the mark of an inferior people, but rather a tenacious and determined people. We are a people who see a scarlet thread called justice in the character of God, which is so strong that it can keep a people focused and a leadership baton passing from generation to generation without wavering.

THE UNIQUENESS OF BLACK PREACHING

In the black religious experience, preaching is an event. Preaching in the black church thrives on the participation of the congregation. Sermons are not unilateral but bilateral. The term *bilateral* refers to the discourse going on between the preacher and the congregation, known as the "call and response pattern." The preacher initiates the conversation, and the congregation answers back with both voice and gestures. For example, when someone in the congregation raises his hand or says, "Go on!" to a point in the sermon, it serves to let the preacher know that the message or impact of his comment was received. The preacher, the Bible, and the congregation are all intertwined in a rich theological interchange.

In addition to the responses from the congregation, the black preacher engages the listeners during the sermon with questions such as, "Can I get a witness?" and "Are you with me?" With each question comes a collective response of affirmation signifying approval, acceptance, and support for his biblical proclamations.

Toward the end of the sermon, the pace will often slow down or speed up. You can tell that the interpersonal atmosphere is about to take a leap into the ionosphere of even deeper communication. The critical juncture comes when he often changes from third-person delivery to first, introducing statements such as, "When *I* think about the cross." The environment is now ripe for an exchange of personal testimony. The preacher shares that not only is the truth of the cross true because it is in the Bible, but it is true because God has borne witness of its monumental impact in the preacher's own life.

Preaching is not just a sermon. Preaching is not simply a transfer of ideology from one man to a group of people. Preaching is a verbal celebration of God and all of His glory. The preacher seeks out the best, most choice words in order to present the truth of the text in a way that propels the hearer into a new realm of discovery and spiritual growth. The preacher not only engages the mind, but also penetrates the very depth of a person's being. It is in that potent combination of delivery that the seeds of transformation embed themselves and take root.

Unfortunately many black seminarians today reduce preaching to an academic exercise. That which has always been natural for the black preacher is often programmed for him in evangelical institutions, with the tragic result being that many exit seminary having lost their ability to preach. Black preaching is thirsty for zest. And the black congregation will demand this zest. If there is not lively, earthy appeal in the sermon, it can become difficult to preach to an African American congregation. And you cannot be an African American preacher and not preach. It is not a fair trade to gain exegetical prowess and lose the ability to maintain a vibrant, engaging connection with your congregation.

The black preacher often focuses on mental retention rather than using notes in the pulpit. This tradition evolved from a couple of factors. The first factor is that his African heritage focused on oral communication and memorization, as I mentioned earlier.

In Africa, storytelling is used to paint pictures of life.[7] The whole culture, its history and its essence, is preserved through oral tradition and celebratory rituals. Stories are also put to melodies and expressed in songs.

Since the Bible is more than two-thirds narrative, the African American preacher is right at home with this type of material. Deuteronomy 6 advocates oral communication as an excellent way to transfer the truth of God to our children. "These words, which I am commanding you today, shall be on your heart. You shall teach them diligently to your sons and shall talk of them when you sit in your house and when you walk by the way and when you lie down and when you rise up" (Deut. 6:6–7). This is similar to African oral tradition, which naturally expressed truth in the normal movement of life. This is why it is still normal to hear black congregations shout back to their pastor during the sermon, "Tell the story," as he powerfully relates Scripture to the black experience.

The second reason the black preacher is tied to oral communication is that for years the black preacher was barred from entering the seminaries, which taught preaching as a technical process. Thus the black preacher simply maintained his heritage, which gave him a great deal of influence in his venue.

The Bible was the first book the slave learned, but in the majority of cases it was not because he could read it. He learned it through what he heard and began interpreting life through it. Even when slavery ended, the Bible remained the black preacher's comprehensive manual on all of life, because he was still denied access to institutions of higher learning. Therefore, African Americans maintained a very orthodox view of Christianity. Our worldview was not tainted by the extraneous and sometimes erroneous thoughts of the American culture.

The interpretational grid for the black preacher's preaching was life. Where biblical truth intersected with life (which is how the Bible was written), the black preacher opened the door to a better life both here and in the hereafter. This type of interpretational model is known as a "language event." As Richard Soulen explains, "A language event can be said to have occurred when reality becomes efficaciously present in language. Here the appearance of 'reality' is identified with the simultaneous coming into being of its 'language.' Without language there is no 'reality.'"[8]

Thus, the black preacher used language to paint pictures relevant to life. He got into the text in order to feel it, experience it, taste it, hold it, embrace it, smell it, and tell it. His words interacted with life's realities and experiences. He saw himself as the Holy Spirit's communicative agent who brought relevant application of the scriptural truths to the lives of the hearers.

There comes a time, however, when it is essential to probe the depths of biblical literature for a more precise meaning, which may lie upon the pages of Scripture beneath the etymology of a certain word or beneath an ancient cultural innuendo.

The drawback in the African American community is that, traditionally, the clergy has not been trained as much to employ the tools of exegesis—lexicons, Greek and Hebrew languages, systematic theologies—which serve as reservoirs of knowledge to link us to the ancient culture. The objective is to obtain the meaning of a given passage.

On the other hand, we cannot camouflage bad expository preaching with Greek and Hebrew words. Academics cannot cover up bad preaching. Neither should the presentation of the truth resemble a documentary on some little-known subject on the Public Broadcasting Station. The best scenario is to fuse the uniqueness of black preaching with strong biblical exegesis. Therefore, the preacher should be both interesting and exacting—offering a relevant exposition of the text. Surely it's a crime to bore people with the Word of God.

As we can see, the language event is a very valuable tool for bringing the Scriptures to life, because it uses life as its interpretive key. But what about all those events and doctrines in the Bible that are alien to our life experience? Formal training is needed to bridge these gaps. The white counterpart of the black preacher had a decided advantage in these areas for a number of years.

Historically, black evangelicalism has sought to take advantage of both worlds. In it, the preacher acquires skills in the area of biblical exegesis, yet maintains the vast riches of our African heritage. African American clergymen need exposure to biblical study, not to make us preachers for such we already are, but to make us better preachers.

Furthermore, when an African American walks onto the campus

of a predominantly white evangelical seminary, it is not as though he brings nothing to the table. He has a wealth of knowledge about preaching and leadership that should be tapped for the betterment of the body of Christ at large. When black evangelicals and white evangelicals come together, it should be a win-win situation. This is why we must graduate from traditional evangelicalism to kingdomology. Kingdomology is *the theological framework and belief system that asserts that God's purpose in history is the manifestation of His glory through the establishment and advancement of His eternal kingdom on earth.* Kingdomology views this purpose as the unifying theme of Scripture that is to be accomplished progressively in history through human instrumentality over and against demonic and human opposition as mankind functions in covenant with Him. This theology finds its ultimate fulfillment in the person, work, and kingdom rule of Jesus Christ (Gen. 1:26–27; Ps. 8:4–6; Ex. 19:5–6; Matt. 6:10, 13; Ps. 22:28).

I had the privilege of participating in this beneficial connection when I taught "Expository Preaching" at Dallas Theological Seminary while completing my doctorate degree. Most of the graduate students I taught were white. While I included exegetical and structural techniques of effective preaching, I also taught stylistic nuances and methods to help broaden the reach of these future white pastors. The students frequently commented that this taught them how to give life, energy, excitement, and relevance to their preaching.

Black preaching is also often set in the context of black church worship, which is formatted from the liturgy of American Christianity. Yet it is African traditionalism that gives the black church and its style of worship the freedom to improvise and innovate.

Henry Mitchell, author of *Black Belief,* saw three primary sources of black hymns and folk songs:

• The slaves commonly quoted biblical texts.

- They quoted white hymns, which also revealed beliefs they held dear and appropriated.
- They restated doctrines of white origin that were highly significant to them.[9]

Music has always had a significant place in the worship of Africans and their descendants. Remember that much of African Traditional Religion was transferred through hymns and songs, which resembled the Psalms of the Old Testament. The music in the black church takes on the form of the Word of God as it is sung. This notion and appreciation for the genre of song is rooted deep within the core of the African heart. Because the orientation toward the ministry of music is set in this vein, the music of the African American church has had a profound impact on the American culture at large. This is why the Negro spiritual has become such a significant part of American life. These songs don't just entertain; they tell the story of life and the people who experienced it. They reveal the unique relationship between the person of God, the oppression of blacks, and the power of faith. These songs were to black people what history books were to whites—our link with our past.

In many cases, the music is a way of drawing people into the black church. Thus a partnership is formed between the pulpit and the choir that results in a unique form of evangelism. Few black preachers allow their sermons to conclude without giving a call to discipleship. The choir sings a song about God's grace, power, and mercy, which softens the heart of the sinner and brings him or her up front before all the church to make a confession of trusting Christ for salvation.

I mentioned earlier that the slaves dressed in their best whenever they came to church. This custom was a carryover from Africa, and can still be experienced in African religious ceremonies today. The worship of God was a celebration. It was a festive event celebrating life, which God both supplied and reigned over. For the slave, the worship service was the only time that he was free. The goodness of God could be celebrated without obstruction. Worship was his reaffirmation of hope. This aspect of celebrating God in worship is still visible in the mainline African American church.

Although slavery has ended, the theme of freedom remains. Where there is hope for freedom, there is much joy and exuberance. This joy and exuberance is evident in the music of the black church, which Henry Mitchell calls a "natural application of the principle of black freedom." He goes on to say, "If the Holy Spirit is assumed to take over the specifics of a prayer or a sermon, why not the details of a musical rendition also? Thus black worship frowns on the meticulous adherence to the printed melodic line."[10]

This mode of celebratory worship is quite biblical. Consider the tenor of Psalm 92, titled, "A Song for the Sabbath day."

> It is good to give thanks to the LORD
> And to sing praises to Your name, O Most High;
> To declare Your lovingkindness in the morning
> And Your faithfulness by night,
> With the ten-stringed lute and with the harp,
> With resounding music upon the lyre.
> For You, O LORD, have made me glad by what You have done,
> I will sing for joy at the works of Your hands.

Many homiletics departments in evangelical seminaries view the emotionalism involved in black liturgy as superfluous. Yet at the core of biblical worship is the recognition of God for who He is, what He has done, and what we are trusting Him to do. We do not see environments where the people passively sit as spectators while the "professionals" perform when we look at the pictures of worship painted throughout the Old Testament, spoken about in the Psalms, and prophesied in heaven in Revelation. Rather, the whole congregation is called to worship God, using every element of expression from shouting to dancing to praising to crying.

Because the Jews of the Old Testament have much in common with the plight of the African American, it is not unreasonable to find similarities between the two styles of worship. Exuberance and joy should not be anomalies in the worship of God. Sacredness does not necessarily imply that we have to be solemn and silent. We are not the "frozen chosen." Of course, silence is appropriate on some occasions (Hab. 2:20), but when the African American considers the care and protection God supplies, especially in light of his socioeconomic plight and history, it is difficult not to be expressive.

Perhaps the same principle is at work in the parable that Christ tells in Luke 7:41–42. In the scene that precedes the parable, the Lord has dined at the house of Simon the Pharisee. At the dinner was a woman whom the Bible refers to as a "sinner" who brought a vial of perfume to anoint Jesus' feet. As she knelt at His feet, "she began to wet His feet with her tears, and kept wiping them with the hair of her head, and kissing His feet and anointing them with the perfume" (Luke 7:38).

It seems that Simon the Pharisee found this type of appreciation to be excessive and improper. Furthermore, this woman was a social outcast. Jesus addressed Simon's insensitivity with a parable in Luke 7:41–43:

> "A moneylender had two debtors: one owed five hundred denarii, and the other fifty. When they were unable to repay, he graciously forgave them both. So which of them will love him more?" Simon answered and said, "I suppose the one whom he forgave more." And He said to him, "You have judged correctly."

When most Anglos observe the worship style of black churches, the mode of worship often seems excessive, just as the woman's actions toward Jesus appeared to be such. But the so-called excessiveness is in proportion to the degree of thankfulness due to the God who has granted forgiveness and a promise of a better life. Therefore, it would be abnormal if we did not render our whole selves to God for the sake of worship. It is this tenet that governs the manner of worship in the black church.

Certainly, black preaching and black worship that overemphasize emotion and performance can be distracting. If we lose our members amid a storm of confusion, "every wind of doctrine" can blow in. Culture is the vehicle, not the driver. The focus of worship must always be the presentation of truth, whether it is sung, taught, or preached. I pray that we may never glorify the package with its pretty wrapping and ignore the precious treasure inside. This is why the African American preacher must be a relevant and excellent expositor as well as a good storyteller.

Today the black preacher remains at the pinnacle of black community leadership, although it is not as high a peak as in days gone by. Because the black church is still the most dominant institution in black America, and because the black preacher is still one of its primary leaders (musical artists now sit side by side), he holds a prominent role as divine representative and cultural leader.

Unfortunately, this role has diminished for a couple of reasons:

The New Diversified Congregation

The black preacher ministers to a more diversified and stratified congregation. In slavery, all were slaves or severely limited by the social limitations of slavery. Not so since the civil rights movement. Diversity of opportunity has led to diversity of expertise. Thus, blacks do not all automatically look to the black preacher for leadership. In fact, a generation of African Americans do not see the church as relevant to their needs, because many pastors have failed to look to, learn from, and adequately use the variety of skills in the black church to address those needs.

Many of these pastors are limited in perspective and understanding of the needs of their contemporary constituency. They are, therefore, unable to address the complex social, economic, familial, and psychological needs and diversity of modern society. To combat this, pastors must take more seriously the apostle Paul's admonition to prepare the saints to do the work of the ministry (Eph. 4:11–12). Failure to adequately recognize and use the expertise of the congregation for the development of the church and the expansion of its ministry to the members and the community will result in increased disillusionment and a decrease in membership and the church's spiritual and social impact in society.

Social Overruling the Spiritual

Another reason for the diminished role of the black preacher is that the spiritual has often taken a secondary role to the social and political in recent times. Far too many issues are fought without concern for biblical methodology, personal salvation, and theological ethics. This is one of the reasons that the success of the civil rights movement was short-lived. Even though laws were changed, hearts were not. Thus, blacks did not experience the internal spiritual changes necessary to sustain the social and political changes. Throughout black church history, personal conversion was at the root of social conversion. This is a diminished priority today, and the progress of the black church and the influence of the black preacher have suffered greatly because of it. This is why social liberation for God's people had to be proceeded by spiritual restoration demonstrated by the day of atonement (Lev. 25).

God is not obligated to bring about social restoration that is not predicated on His standards. Far too many social, political, and economic programs automatically expect black church endorsement and participation simply because of the programs' supposed representation of the black community. These programs want to set the agenda for the church's participation, rather than having the church, based on biblical criteria, establish a kingdom agenda for social change and community empowerment.

Critical Race Theory, for example, must be examined and critiqued based on its conformity to God's Word. Race and racism cannot be the grid for determining theology. Rather, Scripture alone must be the final arbitrator of what is legitimate or illegitimate for this and every other social theory.

In slavery, the black community had to look within itself for meaning, hope, direction, and stability. It drew exclusively from the resources provided by God in order to find the freedom it knew God had granted it. The preacher was the focal point of the community because it could not look outside itself for meaningful leadership. This allowed the black church to rise as a truly independent institution that determined its own direction and destiny under God.

This is tragically not the case today. The African American community has become, to a large degree, a dependent community. In slavery no such dependency existed, because no such dependency was available. The black preacher oversaw a comprehensive institution that clothed the naked, fed the hungry, established businesses, and took care of its orphans. Today many of those responsibilities have been handed over to the state.

Despite the areas of needed improvement, the black preacher still holds a key to the success or failure of the black community's vision of liberation. Just as he provided the comprehensive, qualitative leadership through the most tumultuous times black people have ever faced, he is still poised to accomplish that again as he uses the Bible as his primary manual for hope and freedom.

The fusion of strong biblical exegetical skills with the richly innate prowess of the African American preacher has produced a relevant interpretation of Scripture delivered in a uniquely personal and engaging manner. The shame of the situation is that so few in the body of Christ, outside of African Americans attending African American churches, will experience the full benefit of these insights and discipleship due to the continued separatism that exists within our churches today.

Throughout history, the minority culture(s) integrates into the majority culture in many aspects of life—education, business, and even religion—adopting and adapting to existing cultural norms. However, we should not require legislation in order to recognize and encourage integration among Christian brothers and sisters in the family of God. Especially when there is so much richness and depth of spirituality that can benefit all those who come into contact with it, such as is the case with black kingdomologist preachers today.

I would like to encourage my Anglo brothers and sisters in Christ to, at the least, seek out ways to be discipled and taught by black preachers in the church body—either through books, radio, TV, sermon downloads, or online viewing of sermons. I guarantee that you will be richly fed and go back for more.

But don't stop there. Be intentional in meeting your need for a broader understanding and experience of your faith by looking for ways you can worship and learn under leaders who do not always share your cultural identity or background. Look for African American churches in your area that you cannot only visit, but also attend and even join. Black churches will always have a seat saved for you, since it has always been open to the pursuit of reconciliation in Christ.

Chapter 7

The Black Church and Black Movements

To have historically referred to myself as a black evangelical means that I am a man who has been doubly influenced. On the one hand I have had the distinct mark of the black experience indelibly etched on my life. That means I, like most black baby boomers, have known the good and bad of being black in America. It means I have experienced the ravages of racism while also having partaken of the great history and culture of African American life.

On the other hand, it also means I have been profoundly influenced by white evangelicalism. I have studied in its institutions, interfaced with its church and parachurch organizations, and dialogued with its leadership on its epistemological and theological worldview. I have integrated many of its perspectives and values into my own life and ministry.

It is unfortunate, though, that my appreciation and legitimate pride in my race was not provided to me by my study of Christian theology. Instead, it came as a result of the civil rights movement. It was not until the social revolution of this era that I, like many of my contemporaries, developed a new awareness, appreciation, and awakened self-consciousness of blackness. Until that time I lived in a sort of racial twilight zone. On one side, I was being told that I was created in the image of God and therefore had value. On a pragmatic basis, however, it appeared to me that many of the benefits of possessing that divine image were reserved for white people because it seemed that they were the real benefactors of God's kingdom on earth.

The civil rights movement provided me a new sense of being and significance. As I began to grow my Afro, develop my black salutes, and join in the James Brown refrain, "Say it loud, I'm black and I'm proud," I began to raise deeper questions about the relationship of theology to the issues of race. Questions competed for answers in my mind. What did God have to say about the fact that many Bible colleges, seminaries, and mission organizations would not allow blacks to enter because of our race? What did God have to say about the Bible-teaching Southern Baptist church in Atlanta that would not allow me to participate? Did God have a place for African Americans in His world, or were we an afterthought and second-class spiritual citizens, as appeared to be the case as far as American Christianity was concerned?

This dual reality of race and religion led me and a generation of my contemporaries to examine our theology without simultaneously ignoring or regretting our heritage. The struggle of relating the duplicity in what I was learning theologically from my white professors with what I was experiencing set me on a journey to examine and understand the truth from the Word of God.

In order to comprehend the hybrid nature of black evangelicalism and its implications for American Christianity and the African American church, it is incumbent upon us to understand the themes that led to this distinctive movement within the black church, and continue to shape it today.

Three themes in particular provide the historical, theological, and social backdrop: the conservative nature of the black church, the theological contradiction of the white church, and the influence of the black revolution, contemporary black movements, and the religious consequences.

THE CONSERVATIVE NATURE
OF THE BLACK CHURCH

The black church was *evangelical* long before evangelical arose as an official term. According to *The Evangelical Theological Dictionary*, evangelicalism is the "movement in modern Christianity, transcending denominational and confessional boundaries, that emphasizes conformity to the basic tenets of the faith and a missionary outreach of compassion and urgency."[1]

Theologically, evangelicalism stresses the sovereignty of God as the transcendent, personal, and infinite Being who created and rules over heaven and earth. Furthermore, evangelicals regard Scripture as the divinely inspired record of God's revelation and the infallible, authoritative guide for faith and practice. In addition, the person and work of Christ as the perfect God-man who came to earth as God's means of providing salvation is at the center of the evangelical Christian message.

Given these generally accepted criteria, we cannot speak of evangelicalism and exclude the African American church, which has always held to historic Protestant Christian doctrine. In fact, the black church was founded and then flourished in a conservative biblical tradition. This has been true without regard to denominational affiliation.

More formally, in 1942, J. Elwin Wright was a leading voice in the charge to join with others in establishing the National Association of Evangelicals (NAE).[2] Harold John Ockenga, the first president of the NAE, would later coin the phrase "new evangelicalism" to refer to progressive fundamentalism with a social message.[3]

The evangelical movement (entirely comprised of white theologians at that time) was born out of a need to purge fundamentalism of its sectarian, combative, anti-intellectual, and anti-cultural traits. It also sought to have greater influence by unifying the voices of individual Christians. One of the major focuses was gaining greater radio exposure for preachers, as well as influencing public policy on religious liberties.[4] Nestled under its umbrella were Lutherans, Baptists, Methodists, and others, such as the Assemblies of God. The NAE made slow but steady gains in growth over the years, representing over thirty different denominations and 1.5 million members by 1960.

The official term "black evangelicalism" emerged not long after the NAE's inception out of a call for a clear, articulate biblical theology for the black experience combined with the necessity for a truly evangelical posture toward social issues within the black church.

Thus, black evangelicalism refers to a movement among African American Christians that emerged out of the civil rights era and the rise of evangelicalism in the white community, which seeks to wed the strengths of the black church with an emphasis on a systematic approach to theology, ministry, and social impact.

Yet the white evangelical community did not historically take the African American church seriously. It even encouraged black Christians not to do so either because its theological expression has been an oral tradition, rather than a literary tradition that results in textbooks and formal theological statements.

Given this tendency toward oral expression, we need only to listen to what was preached and prayed and sung.[5] In examining the narratives of Negro history and even the antebellum homilies, it is abundantly clear that the Negro Christian believed the right things about God, the right things about Christ, the right things about the Spirit, and the right things about the Scripture. He did not use the word *omnipotent*; he simply said there's nothing God can't do. The witness of Luke 1:37, "For nothing will be impossible with God," was for the black Christian an all-sufficient statement and was fully credible because Scripture attested to it. The Negro Christian did not talk about the infinity of God, but he knew "God was so high you couldn't get over Him, so low you couldn't get under Him, and so wide you couldn't go around Him," which meant precisely the same thing. He spoke biblical truth in different terminology, but the nature of his theology was evangelical.

Moreover, because blacks were not allowed to attend white schools, they were insulated from the theological controversies of the day, thus limiting the exposure to liberal theology. In the early 1900s, for instance, controversies emerged over the new liberalism, which denied the virgin birth and the inspiration of Scripture.[6] These controversies did not enter into the sphere of black religion because blacks were denied access to the higher evangelical educational institutions where such matters were discussed and debated.

For black Christians caught in a web of oppression and injustice, a much more beneficial enterprise was to formulate a theology of existence and liberation. Other issues were moot and thus deserved a mute response, especially since the formal categories of conservative theology were embedded in the African American community's worldview.

The theologian for the black church was the black preacher. Everything that was pertinent to know about God was articulated in Scripture, and that was his lone authority. If he did not believe his Bible, he could never ascend to the pulpit of the African American church. Because the enslaved black church member also had limited access to formal academic training, members were content to listen to the preacher and measure his credibility against what the Bible said.

The preacher had to be conservative in order to be the preacher. Thus, the black church was sheltered from becoming liberal through the nineteenth century.[7] This began to change, though, as the black church grew in size and scope. The National Baptist Convention, formed in 1895, had over 60 percent of all African American church-goers in its membership. By 1916, that number was nearly three million—making the convention larger than all black religious groups and even larger than the two major white Baptist groups (NBC and SBC).[8] These entities provided a source of stability, strength, and purpose for black people. Excluded from much of the white communities, the black population rose up to provide for our own.

As Henry Louis Gates writes (quoting Anthony Pinn and Evelyn Brooks Higginbotham),

> They (African Americans) were left to make their own way in a segregated world. In their darkest hour, they retreated to the safe space that had always helped them survive oppression: the church. "You have Black churches becoming responsible for so many dimensions of Black life. . . . They are trying to meet a range of needs: educational needs, social needs, economic needs, political needs. The life of Black folks in some very significant ways is being filtered through these organizations. . . . The church has formed a nation within a nation. The church was, then at least, the single most important institution in the Black community."[9]

With this growth in size and scope came a variety of beliefs and values emphases, much of which stemmed from the theological contradictions evident in both the historical and contemporary white church as well as the expansion of basic societal needs to address.

The Theological Contradiction of the White Church

Liberal German rationalism began to infect white churches and their institutions early in the twentieth century. White fundamentalists fought back by establishing alternative religious institutions. These Bible colleges and seminaries sought to train a new generation of youth in conservative theology and prepare them to convert the culture back to God.[10]

As American universities and seminaries became more and more liberal, however, they simultaneously became more and more open racially. Liberal schools led the way in providing religious education to blacks. Conservative schools, on the other hand, were very slow to open their doors.[11] In order to salve their consciences for maintaining the color line, Bible colleges developed separate but equal (most times unequal) evening training programs for blacks, called "Institutes."

Black Christians exposed to these conservative training centers and the ministries that they spawned (such as Youth for Christ, Campus Crusade for Christ, the Navigators, and Young Life) developed a social/theological tension. Although African Americans were being exposed to a systematic approach to understanding the spiritual truths they had always believed, they were also faced with racial segregation, educational disparity, and theological contradictions. As C. Eric Lincoln points out, the existing white theology was a theology singularly lacking in its ability to conceive of humanity beyond the improbable boundaries of the white race—a theology that permitted and sometimes encouraged the sickness of racism and that has on occasion grossly distorted the faith through a calculated attempt to fit the whole of reality into the narrow confines of a doctrine of racial expediency and a deep-seated commitment to a racial manifest destiny.[12]

While white evangelicals nodded their heads toward racial reconciliation through "Race Relations Sundays" and the like, the results were short-lived or superficial at best. In fact, during the season when the black church stood together the most and could have used the support of white evangelical leaders the most, the white evangelical movement kept its distance. "Jerry Falwell gave his 'Ministers and Marches' speech, in which he condemned Martin Luther King Jr. and other ministers engaged in protesting and marching for civil rights, on March 21, 1965, the same day on which King and other black and white ministers were walking across the Edmund Pettus Bridge in Selma, Alabama. Falwell criticized the civil rights movement, declaring that 'preachers are not called to be politicians but soul winners.' He would later apologize for the sermon. . . ."[13]

Black evangelical forerunner Tom Skinner lost considerable influence and support from the white evangelical movement when he addressed the glaring issues in the white Christian movements in a speech titled, "The US Racial Crisis and World Evangelism." Skinner delivered this one-hour talk at the popular InterVarsity Christian Fellowship event called Urbana 70 Student Missions Conference, attended by thousands of white evangelical Christians and roughly four hundred African Americans. In his talk, Skinner stated the following:

> Understand that for those of us who live in the black community, it was not the evangelical who came and taught us our worth and dignity as black men. It was not the Bible-believing fundamentalist who stood up and told us that black was beautiful. It was not the evangelical who preached to us that we should stand on our two feet and be men, be proud . . . and that God could work his life out through our redeemed blackness. Rather, it took Malcolm X, Stokely Carmichael, Rap Brown and the Brothers to declare to us our dignity. God will not be without a witness.[14]

Earlier, he had declared,

> To a great extent, the evangelical church in America supported the status quo. It supported slavery; it supported segregation; it preached against any attempt of the black man to stand on his own two feet. And where there were those who sought to communicate the gospel to black people, it

was always done in a way to make sure that they stayed cool. "We will preach the gospel to those folks so they won't riot; we will preach the gospel to them so that we can keep the lid on the garbage pail."[15]

The same group of people who advocated "the unity of the body" from Ephesians 4:4–6 was also practicing racial disunity. The implicit message was: Let's win their souls, but not value them as people. Unfortunately, this is the exact same sentiment I frequently still hear today. It was even expressed in 2021 by the then newly elected SBC President, Ed Litton, in a national interview aired by CNN centered on discussing racial issues. In the over six minute interview, Ed kept returning to the need to "be about the gospel." He summed up his stance by stating the all-too-familiar "save their souls" motif. He said, "It's basically recognizing that people of color in our communities are created in the image of God . . . it's our mission to help get that gospel message to everybody."[16]

While I fully support and stand behind "being about the gospel" message as a believer in Christ, what I do not want us to neglect in our zeal to take the message of the gospel is our call to simultaneously live out the scope of the gospel as we do. Otherwise we are not walking in line with the truth of the gospel as the apostle Paul stated (Gal. 2:14). The scope of the gospel includes being intentional about racial unity and equity (Gal. 2). When you read Galatians 2, you will clearly see that the apostle Paul called Peter on the carpet on his own racial disunity, saying that he had not been straightforward as to the truth of the gospel (Gal. 2:14). To ignore, dismiss, marginalize, or degrade the ongoing plight of "people of color in our communities" through action, word, or inaction while trying to "save their souls" is a limited view of the scope of the gospel (Ps. 82:3; Isa. 1:17; Mic. 6:8; Matt. 7:12; Matt. 23:23). Racism is a gospel issue because racism is an affront to the truth that all of us are created in the image of

God, and through the salvation of Jesus Christ, become "one new man" in Him. While the content of the gospel gives the believing sinner forgiveness of sins and the free gift of eternal life, the scope of the gospel transforms the personal life and human relationships as it restores human dignity on earth.

Regrettably, not as much has changed over time as we would like to think. As the graduates of these earlier institutions once trekked to the ends of the earth to fulfill the Great Commission of Acts 1:8, they successfully overlooked the Jerusalem, Judea, and Samaria in their own backyard, a focus still prevalent today. In fact, even back then, most mission societies would not even receive black graduates as candidates, whether they were qualified or not, to go "save the souls" of others.

White evangelical theologians understood well the theology of Ephesians 4, but functioned as though these instructions had been given by Immanuel Kant[17] and not the apostle Paul through the agency of the Holy Spirit. It became increasingly apparent that while African Americans could learn systematic formulas for understanding the Bible and theology in these institutions and seminaries, we could only find limited meaningful relationships and empowerment there. Integration came clothed in the isolation of being the lone "black," often viewed as a representation of all black people while at the same time muffled in any real expression of personality or thought. We were allowed in the room, but not given a seat at the table.

It also became evident to most Christian blacks that we were never going to be fully accepted in the broader white evangelical structure throughout the nation. We had been granted a ticket to access another world, but that ticket only opened the door to the stairwell leading to the balcony once again—a balcony rife with the resultant effects of feeling patronized, marginalized, tokenized, and stereotyped. Essentially, integration meant little more than assimilation.

Unfortunately, some black evangelicals thus made the mistake of viewing our own history, culture, and church experience through the lens of white theology. This was a disaster for many as a large number joined whites in assessing Christian blacks as being an "ignorant, uneducated, overemotional group of people." The result of the contradiction within the white church was a contradiction within many Christian blacks as well. This led to an alienation from the very community to whom we had been called to minister and who also had given us birth while supplying us with the rich strengths so greatly needed in the body of Christ at large.

The Influence of the Black Revolution

With the rise of the Negro revolution,[18] which later became known as the black revolution, a community-wide effort developed to change comprehensively the sociopolitical situation in America. Again, the African American church was called upon to provide leadership and cohesiveness to the movement that became a clarion call for identity and empowerment.

An understanding of the black revolution and the subsequent development of a theological and political school of thought is relevant to us not only from an informational standpoint but from an applicational standpoint in how black evangelicalism has been influenced, and at present, why "evangelicalism," and particularly what has come to be known as "white evangelicalism,"[19] has come under fire in a large portion of black Christian culture as nothing more than "Christian nationalism." As Eric Mason explains, "Over the past few years, there's less and less clarity about what it means to be an evangelical. The term has taken on a political agenda that has become disturbing for many."[20]

Mason states elsewhere, "There's so much pain involved with Evangelicalism that the chance to redeem the ideology has lost its fervor. So, now it's kind of like I don't want to redeem the term—I just want to redeem the word 'Christian.' I would rather redeem a word that's in the Bible than a created socio-theological construct which Evangelicalism doesn't realize that it is."[21]

THE BACKDROP OF THE BLACK EXPERIENCE

Comprehending the intricacies behind the emergence and existence of the black revolution can be done only by recalling the backdrop of the black experience. This backdrop cannot be denied and should not be underestimated as to its place in the formation and development of not only the black revolution, but also a political agenda, black power, a theological school of thought, black theology, and an expositional approach to theology and ministry.

All have risen out of the post-slavery fumes rife with racist structures held in place by unwritten and written codes of conduct. Police forces armed to uphold unjust laws as well as fire hoses used to intimidate, crush, or even kill placed the backdrop in a frame of oppression. But as Martin Luther King Jr. bellowed on his last night on earth, "There was a certain kind of fire that no water could put out."[22]

This fire enflamed the African American canvas during the black revolution, igniting it with colors of Afrocentric art, literature, music, and ministry. It was during this period that "Negroes," who were previously known as "colored," became "black." That is, the black community no longer viewed itself in terms of the broader white definitions, but sought to define itself. This new self-consciousness gave rise to everything from new hairstyles and dress to a renewed interest and examination of African history and culture. Black people were going to determine for ourselves who we were and where we were going.

On February 1, 1960, four students from the Negro Agricultural and Technical College in Greensboro, North Carolina, were refused coffee at a local variety store because of their color. In an act of rebellion, they sat at the counter until the store closed. This was the beginning of sit-ins that spread across the South. These protests rested on the heels of the Supreme Court decisions on voting and school desegregation as well as the Montgomery bus boycott.

By the summer of 1960, the status of black Americans had become a burning issue on the national conscience. A growing preoccupation with civil rights had infiltrated every aspect of the black community. By the mid-1960s, large demonstrations across the country began taking place to force the issues of justice and equality and to protest the violence done to blacks. The "white backlash" of the Civil Rights Act of 1964 only increased through violent acts of physical, social, and economic oppression.

An example of this occurred in the life of a man named Amzie Moore. Amzie Moore opened the only black-owned petrol station in the Mississippi Delta around that time. Threats against his life and his family ran rampantly like a broken fuel line flirting with the spark of a society enflamed by subjugation. A rifle leaned against the wall near the rear window, ready to fend off any enraged whites. Guarding, not just managing, his business was a twenty-four-hour job similar in risk to an active-duty soldier on the front lines of a war.

A few years later in the same town of Greenwood, a young man named Stokely Carmichael gave birth to a term for what Amzie, and countless others, had spent his sweat and strength attempting to do. Stokely called it "black power." Stokely had joined with Martin Luther King Jr. and Floyd McKissick (leader of the Congress of Racial Equality) in a Freedom March through Mississippi. This March was originally begun by James Meredith, who was sidelined from the March having been shot by a sniper.

Released from jail for the twenty-seventh time for his involvement with the civil rights movement, Stokely poetically reframed the call to freedom in June of 1966 by declaring that he would not go to jail again. His was no longer a fight for freedom on paper; what he wanted was black power.

Black power called for opportunity to rid oneself of the constraints brought on by an internal imperialism. It called for black businesses to begin, a community of black Americans to unite, and a removal of the dependency caused through indirect rule and psychological and physical oppression. I was sixteen years old when blacks around our nation were urged to redefine ourselves based on our own heritage, values, and goals. Structural sins of separate but unequal segregation, educational disparity, and economic limitation offered no real option of forward progress for an entire group of individuals. On one hand, freedom dangled tantalizingly before us, urging us to pursue all that we knew we could become. Yet when tasted, the carrot came laced with the poison of a prejudicial sociopolitical structure.

Stokely communicated that day in Greenwood that deliverance from a societal system of racism through such things as a Civil Rights Act drafted in pen and ink was not the same thing as freedom itself. Just like the proclamation of liberty etched on the steely side of our nation's bell did little to ensure liberty for all, the Civil Rights Act of 1964, while accomplishing much in ending government discrimination, did little to propel society to follow suit. Deliverance is not freedom. Deliverance is the opportunity to pursue freedom. This opportunity would not be maximized, according to the leadership pointing the way for black liberation in America, apart from a call to empowerment through black power.

The Emergence of Black Theology

A year after giving what black people as a whole had been seeking for hundreds of years—a public and more official name, "Black Power"—riots broke out in Detroit. The Detroit riots of 1967 significantly impacted a young theologian named James Cone. When the riots broke out, Cone was teaching in Adrian, Michigan, at Adrian

College, after having studied at Garrett Theological Seminary and Northwestern University. Having been called to the ministry at the tender age of sixteen, Cone already wrestled with questions concerning his upbringing in Beardon, Arkansas, and its relationship to biblical truth. Was the God of grace that he had learned about at the Macedonia African Methodist Episcopal Church the same God of the roughly eight hundred white people in Beardon who saw him no higher than a servant, and whose church he dared not visit?

Cone later reflected on these days in Beardon by saying that life in his hometown "meant attending 'separate but equal' schools, going to the balcony when attending a movie, and drinking water from a 'colored' fountain. It meant refusing to retaliate when called a n——— unless you were prepared to leave town at the precise moment of your rebellion. You had no name except for your first name or 'boy.'"[23]

Cone's unwavering faith led him to question these inconsistencies. He later summed up his intellectual and spiritual struggles when he wrote,

The conflict between faith and suffering was exacerbated by the fact that most of the brutality inflicted upon black people was done by white persons who also called themselves Christians. Whites who humiliated blacks during the week went to church on Sunday and prayed to the God of Moses and of Jesus. Although blacks and whites expressed their faith in their separate worship services in quite different ways, the verbal content of their faith seemed similar. That was why many blacks asked: How could whites be Christian and yet do such horrible things to black people? And why does God permit white people to do evil things in the name of Jesus Christ?[24]

These existing contradictions, intensified by the urgency of the Detroit riots, redirected Cone's plans to return to graduate school to pursue another PhD, this time in literature at the University of Chicago, which he had intended to use in hopes of altering the national landscape through the power of story. Instead, Cone set out to put in writing a system of theology that spoke to the black experience in America. Cone's immediate vision for his future had changed as he confronted the truth that God could not be indifferent to the inequality he experienced as a child. Nor could God be indifferent to the raping of black women, lynching of black men, burning and bombing of black churches, and the ghettoizing of the minds of black children. The problem was, however, that the classical theological disciplines he had studied in seminary did not speak to those realms. It taught him about existentialism, neoorthodoxy, and fundamentalism. It taught him about the council of Nicaea and the Reformation, but no one was talking, theologically, about the targeted oppression of black people in America.

James Cone concluded that what was needed was a current and more complete way of looking at theology that would emerge out of the dialectic of black history and white culture. The major question he set himself to answer through a study of God's Word was: What has the gospel to do with the black struggle for liberation?

Questions such as this one were raised not only in the spirit of James Cone but in the soul of the black church and community as a whole. They were questions that traditional Christian responses could not answer. Questions included:

How could Christian whites maintain a clear conscience while using their religion to methodically oppress and strip human dignity from African Americans from the time of slavery through the 1960s?

How was God involved in what was taking place within

the society of the oppressed, and what was He sanctioning the black community to do about it?

What would a life no longer dependent on the agencies, government, and other entities of the white power structure look like?

Questions like these echoed in the collective core of the black mind. While evangelicals would do well to listen to James Cone in the areas where he has argued correctly, we must also recognize the areas of disagreement. Primarily, Cone's black theology greatly over-emphasized the black situation of oppression to the point of compromising biblical truth. It also focused heavily on racism to such an extent that no real basis for reconciliation was afforded. Likewise, Cone's interpretation of the relationship of Jesus Christ to liberation failed to integrate it into the whole of God's salvific purpose for mankind.

It became common to hear black people referring to Christianity as a "white man's religion" that failed to address the sum total of experiences, institutions, actions, mentality, and conditions that affected black people in their journey from slavery onward. White religion did not recognize that to grow up black in the structures and definitions of a white-dominated society is distinctly different from growing up white. Without that awareness, there resulted a failure to ascertain the participation of God in the framework of black life.

Black theologians no longer spent time addressing epistemological issues as they had been taught to do for so long, but rather a focus shifted in the black conscience to the ethical outworking of the orthodox epistemological conclusions. Rejecting the concept that Christ was concerned with the black soul while ignoring black oppression, Christian leaders influenced by the black revolution sought to define a biblical, holistic theology of hope. A nascent awareness arose for the need to develop a unified thrust to bring about true liberation, and not only a spiritual liberation that will be realized upon reaching heaven.

This component of theological clarification presented the option of a more biblically sound and socially relevant eschatology to that existing in the realm of white theology. Earth, rather than heaven, became the major focus of the church. Having a previous eschatological emphasis on the future had been a common thread throughout African American Christianity, given to it by the teaching of those who sought to subdue any hint of autonomy against them. Wrestling with these and other issues, James Cone wrote,

> White missionaries persuaded most black religious people that life on earth was insignificant because obedient servants of God could expect a reward in heaven after death. As one might expect, obedience meant adherence to the laws of the white masters. Most black people accepted the white interpretation of Christianity, which divested them of the concern they might have had about their freedom in the present.[25]

This perspective changed as a result of the black revolution. Songs such as "We Shall Overcome" replaced heaven-only-focused spirituals such as "I Know the Other World Is Not Like This." A shift was made to no longer wait for a New Jerusalem, but to also strive toward the creation of new cities in the here and now. Eschatology was no longer viewed as an escape hatch that allowed the believer to live without taking seriously the need for helping to shape the earth into what it ought to be. What was not being presented was an idealistic view that this task would be accomplished entirely, for that won't be done until Christ comes back. However, what was being raised at this time in the minds of black theologians was that the church had the responsibility to demonstrate God's justice and righteousness in the world now.

Toward this end, in June of 1969, what came to be known as the "theological arm" of black power was released in a "Statement by the National Committee of Black Churchmen." This statement, largely authored by Cone, set in motion the public intellectual structure already innate in black culture, while giving it the name of black theology. It read,

> Black Theology is a theology of black liberation. It seeks to plumb the black condition in the light of God's revelation in Jesus Christ, so that the black community can see that the gospel is commensurate with the achievement of black humanity. . . . The message of liberation is the revelation of God as revealed in the incarnation of Jesus. Freedom is the gospel. Jesus is the Liberator![26]

Black theology did an essential job in raising and addressing crucial questions that for too long had been overlooked by white American Christianity. It awakened the American theological world to the reality that oppression is an evil affront against God's person and activity in history. It affected the black church profoundly, propelling it forward toward a greater understanding and ability to look after community needs effectively. It reminded all people that theology must find a relevant demonstration in society, that the God of the Bible is not too highly removed that He is not also a God of everyday miry and mucky realities, and that His heart for the suffering and for the poor should be our own.

The black revolution had given rise to a political and theological revolution in black power and black theology that attempted to wrap its systematic arms around the relationship of Scripture to the experience of what it means to be black in America. Concerns were addressed in order to construct an interpretation of Scripture in light of the black experience that spoke to the black soul. Students of the

Bible sought to find an integrating point between the oppressed condition of the black community as a whole and the God who is at work freeing the oppressed.

A proper understanding of the black revolution, black power, and black theology is not simply helpful from a historical vantage point, but for contemporary application as well in our church and society at large. Health care reform, immigration reform, bailouts, stimulus packages, climate control, voter suppression, economic disparity, cancel culture, criminal justice reform, and police reform headline the current debate between capitalism and socialism.

This, and other like issues, have been served on the table of contemporary relevance, reemerging to dominate every major news station while becoming the topic of choice around water coolers, on social media, and in our church lobbies. In 2008, fueled by the fiery words of an even more fiery preacher named Jeremiah Wright in support of the election of our first African American president, Black Liberation Theology was reawakened as a sleeping giant ready to ask everyone who has ears to hear: How far have we come? The answer to that question varies depending on who steps up to address it but it is a question that has only gained momentum in its asking and need to be addressed, especially over the last few years with the continual rise of a focus on Critical Race Theory, systemic racism, NFL players' national anthem protests, divisions within Christendom and large denominations such as the Southern Baptist Convention, and an exodus from evangelicalism en masse.

CONTEMPORARY BLACK MOVEMENTS

On May 25, 2020, the racial conflict in America rose to a whole new level with the very public murder of George Floyd. His death brought about by a white police officer kneeling on his neck was filmed on a cellphone for the world to see. It ignited a racial firestorm throughout America and beyond. Floyd's death was the proverbial straw that broke the camel's back. People black, white, and brown took to the streets in protest, lament, and grief over a past whose effects, both covert and overt, are yet to be addressed or healed.

And while data can demonstrate differing assertions on whether blacks face a higher amount of police brutality than whites or not, the historical root embedded within the systems remains in the DNA of our core. For those who felt that the national outcry of peaceful protests and lamenting displayed online (not the riots) were too much of a display for a man who was a former criminal, let NFL player Benjamin Watson's words help you to understand the collective feeling when we saw what we did. Watson writes,

> White people have no idea of the fear that black people feel toward the police. I cannot say that strongly enough, loudly enough, or forcefully enough. I believe it is a huge point of division between black people and white people. Black people have little expectation of being treated fairly by police in any situation. We have a high expectation of being demeaned, abused, and possibly treated violently in any encounter with law enforcement. We have a history that supports this, news headlines that shout this, and personal experiences that confirm this. This is a reality that white people simply don't know.[77]

We need to be careful to keep in mind that while the statistics certainly support that every issue in our nation is not "race-based," nor are the laws overtly enforcing racist structures anymore, the sensitivities are still there because of our shared history. This can feel like systemic racism or racism, even if intentions may not be. We would do well to be compassionate to these sensitivities in others rather than dismiss them out of hand because we may not agree with their conclusions.

The heartbreaking and stark visual of police brutality that May day in Minnesota catapulted this pain to the public arena on full display. The discourse of social justice dominated our conversations more than it had in a long time, posing questions of: What is it, and who is responsible to carry it out? One such group that stepped forward to address these questions was Black Lives Matter.

BLACK LIVES MATTER

The focus and support of the mantra "Black Lives Matter" is legitimately born out of tragedy. It originally came to a more formalized structure in 2013 and rose on the national scene after the events of Ferguson, Missouri, and Michael Brown's death.[28] It rose to global prominence after the death of George Floyd. The movement highlights the injustices against black lives in much the same way that white evangelicals emphasize that the lives of unborn babies matter.

The Black Lives Matter movement essentially has two aspects. There is the informal movement by those who stand up for injustice against black lives, using peaceful protests and education to bring about healthy cultural and police reforms. There is also the official organization, trademarked as Black Lives Matter, and founded by Patrisse Cullors (who has since resigned amid controversy), Alicia Garza, and Opal Tometi. The formal entity of Black Lives Matter advocates key elements of an agenda that cannot be supported by serious Christians. It rejects the primacy and protection of the nuclear family while promoting the acceptance of gay and transgender lifestyles.[29] In addition, the founders openly embrace an ideological framework of Marxism, an anti-theistic movement.[30]

The Black Lives Matter *focus* has merit in the overarching mission of social injustice for black lives in particular, an oft-overlooked aspect of social reform. But like all social *movements*, Black Lives Matter must be examined, analyzed, and critiqued against the backdrop of God's inerrant Word.

CRITICAL RACE THEORY

In the wake of the collective upheaval taking place, the Black Lives Matter movement also gave fresh legs to Critical Race Theory, which now stands tall at the core of today's racial debate. I want to explore CRT more fully since it seems to dominate the interviews, talk shows, and dialogue in much of our nation at the time of this writing.

Unfortunately, it seems as though there are as many definitions for CRT as there are people discussing it. You might understand a bit better if I were to compare it to fireworks exploding on the 4th of July. Fireworks are shot up into the air and burst into a million separate flames. They start off as solid but once the explosion occurs, it all spreads in a variety of different directions. You can no longer see what was originally launched because what was originally launched has exploded.

This is what has happened to the issue of race in America, and to Critical Race Theory in particular. An explosion has occurred from an original theory that left everybody asking, "What in the world is CRT, anyhow?" It's become hard to find a definition of it that everyone seems to understand or agree upon because of the explosions that have taken place (the iterations and various nuances). So, I'll define CRT succinctly for our discussion at hand by giving you what many of the originators say it is, or was intended to be, when it was created.

Critical Race Theory may be defined as a post-civil rights social theory that demonstrates how unjust laws have served as the embedded foundation and filter through which racist attitudes, behavior, policies, and structures have been rooted and continue to influence the fabric of American life, politics, and systems, even after those laws were changed.

CRT proponents view race as a social construct created to expand or protect power and control. It also holds that the foundation of society's institutions and power structures are based on white privilege. Proponents frequently contend that these institutions and structures are inherently racist in that they are consciously or subconsciously used to maintain and expand the economic and political power of white people at the expense of people of color.[31] Proponents of CRT also contend that storytelling and narrative-based knowledge is a leading element in changing cultures, affecting worldviews, and even addressing systemic issues. One of the leading CRT theorists, Kimberlé Crenshaw, defines it as "a way of looking at law's role platforming, facilitating, producing, and even insulating racial inequality in our country."[32]

Never has there been a more volatile subject separating schools, school boards, churches, denominations, organizations, businesses, and even personal relationships through heated emotions and often verbal vitriol. Which is also why I have chosen to examine more fully the historical definition by those who created it to offer context to the conversations at hand. In his own words, one of the founders of CRT, Derrick A. Bell Jr.,[33] said it is

> a body of legal scholarship . . . a majority of whose members are both existentially people of color and ideologically committed to the struggle against racism, particularly as institutionalized in and by law. Those critical race theorists who are white are usually cognizant of and committed to the overthrow of their own racial privilege.[34]

CRT is said to have germinated as early as the 1960s and 1970s but more formally in the late 1980s, according to Angela P. Harris.

She writes that it came about as a mixture of Critical Legal Studies (founded in Wisconsin in 1977) and civil rights scholarship, in hopes of revitalizing "scholarship on race" and correcting the "deconstructive excesses of CLS."[35] Angela writes, "CRT's ultimate vision is redemptive, not deconstructive."[36]

While having ties to Critical Legal Studies, CRT has its own distinctions, particularly regarding approaches to reform as well as caution toward liberal policies. One of the founders, law professor Patricia Williams, emphasizes a key difference "when she acknowledges as example that the paper-promises of enforcement packages like the Civil Rights Act of 1964 have held out as many illusions as gains."[37] Essentially, this difference points out that while laws preventing and prohibiting systemic racism as well as promoting racial equality were passed and enacted by our government (an intended outcome for followers of CLS), due to the underlying nature inherent in culture and collective thought, the positive outcomes of these laws didn't always come to pass.[38]

Critical Race Theory gained its official standing in 1989 in Wisconsin at the first annual workshop on Critical Race Theory. According to historian Ibram X. Kendi, "Several dozen legal scholars met at a convent outside of Madison, Wisconsin, on July 8, 1989, as Public Enemy's 'Fight the Power' topped Billboard charts. They came together to forge an anti-racist intellectual approach known as *critical race theory*. Thirty-year-old UCLA legal scholar Kimberlé Williams Crenshaw organized the summer retreat the same year she penned 'Demarginalizing the Intersection of Race and Sex.'"[39]

Kendi continues, "Derrick Bell, Alan Freeman, and Richard Delgado, the early formulators of *critical race theory* in law schools, were also in attendance at the 1989 summer coming-out party for *critical race theory*. One of the greatest offshoots of the theory was critical Whiteness studies, investigating the anatomy of Whiteness, racist ideas, White privileges, and the transition of European immigrants into Whiteness. Critical race theorists, as they came to be called, joined anti-racist Black Studies scholars in the forefront of revealing the progression of racism in the 1990s."[40]

Critical Race Theory, much like Critical Legal Studies, focused on how systems served the interests of the wealthy and powerful. But Critical Race Theory differed from Critical Legal Studies in that it did not fully embrace political liberalism, seeing liberalism as unable to truly rectify issues of injustice in society. Professor Derrick Bell stated in his lecture entitled "Who's Afraid of Critical Race Theory?" that CRT's "writing and lecturing is characterized by frequent use of first person, storytelling, narrative . . . and the unapologetic use of creativity. The work is often disruptive because its commitment to anti-racism goes well beyond civil rights, integration, affirmative action and other liberal measures." Bell went on to say that CRT's adherents "are highly suspicious of the liberal agenda, distrust its method, and want to retain what they see as a valuable strain of egalitarianism which may exist despite, but not because of, liberalism."[41]

CRT contends that racism has embedded itself in schools, curricula, law enforcement, the legal system, the military, corporations, target marketing, districting, medical industries, infrastructure, and civil government. CRT holds that the virus of racism has comprehensively infected the entirety of American society and must, as a result, be comprehensively addressed.

Three prominent features of CRT involve *whiteness as normative*, *interest conversion* (also known as *convergence theory*), and *intersectionality*. I go into *whiteness as normative* previously in this book, but essentially it refers to a mindset that places the "white perspective" as the normative perspective to view all things. It is the grid through which human attributes and behaviors are measured, using whiteness as the "neutral" cornerstone and standard. Also, briefly, *interest conversion* was brought to public discourse in 1980 when professor Derrick Bell analyzed why *Brown v. Board of Education* was decided favorably for blacks in 1954 as opposed to any other time period previously in which it had ardently been fought for. His assessment was that this period of time lent itself to desegregation because the white population in power wanted to reduce the threat of internal disruption and rebellion by returning black veterans who had fought alongside white soldiers for the concept of "freedom" in the Korean War. In addition, they wanted to facilitate economic development in the South, which was, at that point, being stifled by segregation. In his own words, "the interests of Blacks in achieving racial equality will be accommodated only when it converges with the interests of Whites."[42]

Intersectionality is the view that an oppressive reality can intersect or connect with other forms and sources of oppression (i.e., class, gender, language, disability) that then places a person at risk of experiencing multiple forms of trauma and oppression. It argues that an individual's social or personal experience combines to produce different "intersections" of either discrimination or privilege, but that this happens to a greater degree in the lives of the marginalized and poor.

These are not the only features in CRT but they are three of the most discussed currently, and which you may have heard or be familiar with. CRT proponents often declare that white supremacy, white power, and white privilege are at the root of our nation's historical and contemporary social ills. Writings or lectures frequently claim that this embedded racism is overtly seen in things like police brutality, the effects of redlining, and gerrymandering. They purport that racism is also passive-aggressively manifested in microaggressions. *Microaggressions* involve the sending of racially coded messages, denigrating messages, and actions that insult, stereotype, dismiss, or demean others—minority ethnic groups in particular, but it can also apply to other subgroups like the disabled or "English as a Second Language" speakers.

CRT proponents state that even though many of the unjust laws were changed, the systems had already been infiltrated with the previous disparities and prejudices. In this way, the effects of those laws did not automatically, and to varying degrees through today, change with it. So, the fruit (like Adam's sinful fruit manifest in humanity) of unrighteous laws still express themselves in the structures of our contemporary society. One argument of CRT today is that many people still have to struggle with the issue of racism, not because it's a law, but because we live in an environment that was affected by unjust laws, and its ripples still reach our shores.

Take, for example, the law established in the 1930s known as *redlining*.[43] This law was created in order to segment populations by location. It's called *redlining* because zones that were drawn in red indicated a hazardous community environment. A hazardous community meant that mortgages would not be loaned out to home buyers. It meant that businesses would not invest in the development of the area. It meant many things. But what it meant the most was that a certain segment of society found themselves stuck in the Red Line Districts. Generations were born into those districts, allowing for the repercussions of the redlining to be transferred from one generation to another. They were, by and large, locked out of segments of society that would have allowed them better opportunities to advance.

At this time, redlining laws do not exist based on race. But that does not mean the influence of those laws do not affect people today due to continuing existing redlining mentalities and worldviews. Many people were never able to get out of these zones due to poor education, unstable environmental exposure, economic deprivation, poor education, and an inability to see beyond the red line drawn in the sand.

Lines have been drawn today as well. Different lines. Lines between people of all political, social, racial, and educational differences regarding the legitimacy of these movements and social theories that seek to highlight generational disenfranchisement. Debates rage concerning to what degree they should be taught, funded, resisted, or rejected outright.

While I contend that some of the observations and approaches of CRT are rooted in truthful historical analysis as it seeks to address the insidious racism carried out through overt and covert words and actions, as well as the ineffective policies enacted under the banner of "colorblind" laws of the past and present, its foundation is wrong. I say that its foundation is wrong because the grid on which it exists is based on a sociological perspective rather than a theologically sound kingdom agenda worldview. While racism is an evil sin severely condemned by God, it is neither the first sin, the only sin, nor the defining classification of sin. Idolatry, which is always rooted in pride, is the superintending sin in Scripture. Racism is certainly one major humanistic evil expression of the sin of idolatry since it is an attack on the value of the image of God in which all mankind of every ethnicity is created. On the other hand, the debate on the legitimacy of CRT should not be used for ignoring or shutting down legitimate interaction on the ongoing problem of race and racism in America. It also should not be used to limit the teaching on the authentic history of our nation.

While I agree that teaching a revisionist history of solely oppressed/oppressor constructs should not be the approach, I do believe we need to tell history in its comprehensive truthful context. We are not to marginalize it. We are not to whitewash it. We are to tell and teach the truth; the whole truth. Slavery was horrible. Jim Crow was horrific. More than 4,500 men were lynched, most often on trumped-up charges never proven with due process. We are to teach about towns such as Rosewood, Florida, being completely destroyed until there was no town left at all—illegitimate revenge killings on charges, once again, not given due process. People both black and white need to know about the evil practice of criminal leasing that used the illegitimate incarceration of black men to force them into economic servitude for the benefit of white greed. We are to teach that the town of Rosewood stood as a beacon of black business success where every business was owned and operated by blacks, except for one—until the town was burned down. We are to teach about Black Wall Street in Tulsa, Oklahoma, and how it was annihilated. We are to teach about how every pocket of progress blacks began to achieve as a group was swiftly met by a new form of oppression or targeted dismantling. I could go on and on. We are not to skip true stories, no matter how ugly or painful they are. We are not to pretend they are not history because they don't fit the popular view of our nation. We are to teach the truth, in large part so we don't repeat it. And also so we can work together to heal from it and undo its lasting legacies of destruction showing up so often today in other ways.

We also, however, are to major on teaching, emphasizing, celebrating, and highlighting the massive number of black achievements that injustice was not able to extinguish. People of all races need to learn from the historical faith-based strength of black America, that in spite of slavery, segregation, and injustice we not only persevered but also helped to build and promote the social, political, economic, and religious advancement of the entire nation, enabling it to reach the level of greatness that it has obtained.

Much of the criticism of CRT arising within the black community and Christian leaders comes from the need for a greater emphasis on personal responsibility to secure upward mobility, as well as a desire for a greater focus on preserving the black family. Voddie Baucham summarizes these sentiments when he writes what so many of us believe: "This connection between stable families and the rule of law is something most of us know intuitively. It doesn't mean that we have a simplistic understanding of racism or deny it exists. It just means that we understand the importance of the family as it relates to the community at large."[44] As goes the family, so goes the culture.

On these and many issues, black biblicists—having shared the same experience and therefore the same concerns that the black revolution, black power, black theology, and other black movements addressed—offer that our answers are in line with a commitment to an exegetical and expository approach to Scripture. Historically, black evangelicals were never fully members of the black revolution, although we supported and identified with the call and need for social justice. But neither were we fully members of white evangelicalism, although we benefited from many of its structures of study, ministries, and approaches to theology.

This reality formed a distinction in our approach within both the black church and the broader American evangelical church, providing a unique impetus for the systematizing of a theology on discipleship, oneness, and social justice that is rooted and grounded in biblical truth. This is why I believe that, in time, more and more believers will be identifying as "kingdomologists" instead of "evangelical," no matter what their race is. Kingdomology retains the original emphasis that once proved real in evangelicalism of biblical justice, social focus, and scriptural integrity, but distances itself from the spiritual superiority, nationalism, and divisiveness that has recently overtaken and, in many ways, consumes contemporary evangelicalism.

Chapter 8

The Rise of Black Evangelicalism and Kingdomology

S everal influencing factors led to the rise of black evangelicalism as a movement in the black church in the mid to late 1900s. First, many "colored" institutes, previously established by fundamentalists in order to maintain both a spiritual and a social segregation at the educational level while still offering biblical training, began to adopt an evangelical approach to the study of Scripture, which included addressing social issues. Second, white evangelical schools started to open their doors, albeit slowly, to black students, which afforded blacks the opportunity to study in evangelically minded institutions. Third, a number of white parachurch organizations began to intentionally recruit African Americans to join their staff in order to broaden the ministry's perspective on how to reach the black community. And fourth, evangelical Bible teaching spread through the medium of Christian radio, providing broad-based exposure to a number of individuals who would not otherwise have had the opportunity to experience it.

Christian blacks exposed to evangelicalism realized that if they were going to prioritize the evangelization and discipleship of black America successfully while remaining culturally and socially sensitive and relevant, they were going to have to unite for the purpose of ministry. So in 1963 a group of black leaders formed the National Negro Evangelical Association (NNEA), the first distinctively black evangelical organization.

The NNEA became the primary information center for black evangelical outreach, fellowship, theological debate, and ministry exposure. It concerned itself with a commitment to the authority of the Scripture, a burden for the spiritual state of black America, the need for oneness in the body of Christ, and the application of the gospel to the issue of social justice.

Although a distinctive movement, the NNEA did not entirely abandon its denominational affiliations, because black evangelicals needed to be where black people were—in the black church. Maintaining a relationship with the black church was crucial because of the need to maintain black culture from an evangelical perspective. Through organizations such as the NNEA, which later was renamed the National Black Evangelical Association (NBEA), black evangelicalism entered the structures of American society on two fronts: first, through the establishment of independent black evangelical churches, and second, as an expansion into the existing black denominational structures.

Recognizing the strengths and weaknesses in both the black and white churches in America, pastors and theologians in black evangelicalism sought to simultaneously build the strengths of both while addressing the weaknesses of both. This provided the church at large with a greater holistic approach to the topics studied in the Bible and theology, and it provided the black church with a more refined systematic approach to understanding Scripture and its contemporary application.

THE FATHERS OF BLACK EVANGELICALISM

Scores of talented men paved the way for the inception and spread of black evangelicalism. The pages of this book are not enough to do

justice to them all. However, a few men stand in need of special rec-
ognition as fathers to those of us who followed them. These include
Dr. John Perkins, Rev. Tom Skinner, Dr. William Bentley, Dr. B. Sam
Hart, and Dr. Ruben Conner.

Dr. John Perkins

In 1970, black students leaving a protest in Mendenhall, Mississippi, were rounded up by police, beaten, and taken to prison. This
was done as a setup to bait a man named John Perkins who had spent
his life as a preacher and social activist, leading protest marches and
boycotts against unjust laws, as well as ministering to the poor. When
John arrived at the jail to argue for the release of the students, he was
immediately surrounded by twelve cops, who searched him and then
dragged him into the longest night of his life.

On this night, holed up in a dark room with paintless walls and
a concrete floor, John was beaten, bound to a chair, battered with
leather blackjacks, and then, after hours of abuse, even forced to
wipe up his own blood. Afterward, seeing John drift between a loss
of consciousness and a state of physical shock, most of the other
prisoners did not think that he would make it through the night.
But God spared his life. John remembers a prayer he prayed during
the extreme escalation of his pain. He prayed, *Lord, if You will let me
survive this, I will devote my life to bringing the races together in love
and service to You.*

Not only did John Perkins survive the night, but he went on to
lead the way toward unity in America, earning him the affectionate
title "the godfather of racial reconciliation." Dr. Perkins personally
challenged me on a number of occasions to commit myself to the
study of Scripture and the carrying out of its principles toward reconciliation and empowerment among the Christian communities
of America.

Reverend Tom Skinner

Rev. Tom Skinner initially arose as an evangelist on the national platform. A former Harlem gang member, Tom dedicated his life to God late in his teen years. As early as the age of twenty, he was drawing crowds and conversions through his ability to present the gospel in a compelling yet clear manner. As Skinner grew spiritually, he became a powerful evangelist who shared the gospel for over thirty years and in more than seventy different countries. He was also the chaplain for the Washington Redskins and served as a team motivator for other professional sports teams. He established a high technology learning center that served the inner city and the Skinner Leadership Institute, which provided networking, bridge building, and leadership development.

Tom's success opened doors for him within both the white and black worlds. As these doors opened, Tom addressed the contradiction of the white church and the black experience by bringing a kingdom mindset to the forefront. However, as Tom became more engaged with the white church, he witnessed a level of hypocrisy within it that made him uncomfortable. He saw firsthand an unwillingness to deal with racial, social, and economic injustices.

Tom began to speak openly and courageously about these issues in an era when that wasn't done, and as a result he ended up experiencing rejection from many of the Christian whites who had been supporting him. Radio stations found his messages to be too "controversial" and often stopped playing them. These issues propelled Tom even more deeply into challenging the body of Christ to *be* the body of Christ in both truth and in form. Nearly all influential black conservative leaders today will point to Tom Skinner, with his fiery commitment to the kingdom and social justice, as a father to them in their own ministry.

I met Tom Skinner through Dr. B. Sam Hart. Skinner was a true bridge builder, seeking reconciliation and breaking down dividing walls of age, economic status, race, and religion. He emphasized social justice and racial reconciliation, but he did so by presenting the gospel and accentuating the kingdom of God. He had the unique ability to communicate with every age and cultural group—something that he helped teach me. I could not comprehend why the church should just be spiritual while neglecting the social, or why social activism should be done (as it was so often done) absent a sound theology integrated in and through the local church. Skinner helped me formulate a balanced view of the gospel. His ministry of hope, renewal, and reconciliation changed the lives of thousands of people, and for that, he will forever be remembered in a position of honor among Christian historians.

Dr. B. Sam Hart

Another father in the early inception and spread of black evangelicalism was Dr. B. Sam Hart, who founded the Grand Old Gospel Fellowship ministry (GOGF), which sought to plant churches, prepare leaders, and proclaim the gospel through tent crusades, broadcast media, and overseas long- and short-term missions. GOGF also trained pastors in third-world countries and ministered through orphanages.

B. Sam Hart forever changed my life. He is the man who challenged me to go into full-time Christian ministry, and he also encouraged me to attend Bible college, something that I was not considering at the time. Furthermore, when I was seventeen years old, Dr. Hart invited me to travel to Guyana, South America, to help set up a gospel crusade.

In Guyana, I met my wife, Lois, for the first time. I spent one month in Guyana, but I told Lois that I was going to return as soon as I could to marry her. A year and a half later, I kept my promise. In fact, Lois would go on to work for Dr. Hart and the ministry in helping to duplicate ministry tapes shortly after we married. This, along with her later work at the Billy Graham Evangelistic Association, prepared her for her future role of helping me to start our broadcast ministry, The Urban Alternative, and later to help run it as the Executive Vice President. There would be no Evans family, national ministry, or legacy without Dr. Hart's influence.

However, this isn't fully why he should be honored. Dr. Hart was a faithful black evangelist who emphasized biblical literacy and church planting. He not only impacted my life, but he introduced innumerable souls to Jesus Christ and helped them to grow in their faith.

Through his untiring work, Dr. Hart established black evangelical churches outside of traditional black church structures, strongly emphasizing a call to sound biblical theology connected with a strong emphasis on personal evangelism. He emphasized the need for evangelical Bible teaching in these churches. Through his influence, a church-planting movement was spawned on the East Coast. In addition, Dr. Hart was one of the first black evangelicals to gain a platform in the broader media through his weekly radio broadcast.

Dr. William Bentley

Dr. William Bentley was one of the leading architects of the NNEA. He possessed a strong theological desire for the evangelical movement among blacks to reveal how to emphasize the Bible and theology while also addressing racism, segregation, and oppression. Dr. Bentley was a keen black historian as well as an astute black theologian. One of the highlights that I looked forward to in every NNEA convention in the 1970s and '80s was the debates he and I held concerning how to marry the legitimate strengths of black theology's emphasis on the black experience and black liberation with the evangelical emphasis on the authority of Scripture.

Dr. Ruben Conner

Dr. Ruben Conner established Black Evangelist Enterprise (formerly known as Black Evangelistic Enterprises) in Dallas, Texas, which was a church-planting organization designed to bring about a greater emphasis of Bible teaching to black churches in America. Dr. Conner is considered one of the fathers of the contemporary independent urban church-planting movement in America.

In 1931, Dr. Conner was born in a typical African American farming community, which suggested he would become nothing more than a third generational farmer. On top of that, his mother died shortly after he was born, and his father remarried seven times. Dr. Conner dropped out of school in the seventh grade.

However, God had a different plan for his life. Dr. Conner joined the military when he was sixteen. After seven years of service, a Bronze Star, and combat injuries, he returned home before moving to Dallas. He converted to Christianity, got married, and opened his barber shop where he began evangelizing and preaching. He then earned his GED, attended Bible school, and made history in 1960 when he planted the first African American Bible Church in the South.

Dr. Conner, who later earned two master's degrees and a doctorate degree, served as the senior pastor at Community Bible Church for twenty-five years. He also launched Black Evangelistic Enterprises, which helped establish over forty evangelical churches worldwide—including the church I have served as senior pastor for more than forty-five years, Oak Cliff Bible Fellowship.

While at DTS, I began attending Community Bible Church where Dr. Conner pastored. After being accepted as the first African American into the DTS doctoral program, I was also invited to become an associate professor. However, Dr. Conner, along with some others, challenged me to start a Bible church in Dallas under Black Evangelistic Enterprises as a way of modeling the ideas that I had for connecting the spiritual and social state of my community. There would be no Oak Cliff Bible Fellowship, where I pastor, without Dr. Conner.

Dr. Conner was a faithful preacher, pastor, mentor, and church planter who emphasized social change in African American culture. He not only impacted my life, but he impacted innumerable souls for the kingdom.

THE FUNDAMENTALS OF BLACK EVANGELICALISM

The presence of a black evangelical emphasis provides a number of distinctions that enhance the overall well-being and comprehensive depth and kingdom perspective of Christianity both in America and abroad. This is due to the convergence of the existing major theological tenets present in contemporary biblical Christianity with a concern for the oppressed as well as the social realities of the black experience. Some of these distinctions include the primacy of biblical authority, the priority of racial reconciliation, the importance of personal responsibility, the prominence of biblical justice, and the responsibility for personal evangelism and need for formal discipleship. Let's take a look at a few and then conclude this book with a final look at where things stand today.

The Primacy of Biblical Authority

There is a vast difference between learning from the past and living in it. While black theology should not be undervalued or ignored as far as it raised and sought to address essential issues within the black experience, the foundational interpretational grid for black theology rested more in experience than in exposition.

Volumes have been written as a critique to black theology as well as the distinction of black evangelicalism. My own ThD dissertation is titled "A Biblical Critique of Selected Issues in Black Theology." I don't intend, nor do I have the space, to adequately address all of the various systems of thought within black theology and black evangelicalism. And while the term is under attack, for the purposes of explaining its history and impact, I will use it throughout. I want to emphasize a major differentiating factor between black theology and black evangelicalism, and that is the approach to interpreting Scripture. I have termed the two varied approaches "black experiential theology" and "black expositional theology."

In an attempt to relate the condition of black people to the teaching of Scripture, black theology elevated the black experience to such a degree so as to impose itself on Scripture, making "blackness" the criteria for true interpretation. This incorrectly elevated the issue of contemporary context above the overall overwhelming issue of revelation. Consumed by the liberation motif, this faulty control given to a culturally conditioned theme gave rise to a school of thought that made the Bible the servant of culture, history, and experience.

This produced a more anthropologically centered theology, since social liberation was made the governing hermeneutical principle through which all of the Scripture is to be interpreted. Biblical subpoints became theological categories, thus giving them a place of preeminence they were never meant to have. Black theology emphasized an experiential revelation to varying degrees from theologian to theologian; however, it is safe to say that a basis of experiential interpretation served as its underpinning.

Black evangelicalism, on the other hand, views Scripture as the standard for judging the black experience. The ultimate goal of revelation, whether general or special, is Godward. It is designed to bring all people into harmony with who God is and what He is about. History is crucial to revelation because God is revealing Himself in time and space, and liberation is an important activity of God in history. However, the extraction of the social liberation motif from history as the superintending sufficient revelation of God's activity in history is incorrect because it makes the human situation rather than the divine revelation its ultimate end.

When studying Scripture, the question that any group must ask is whether knowledge of God and the advancement of His kingdom is the goal. To have any other goal is to make Scripture the hand-maiden of humanity. No human experience bears divine authority in and of itself. Neither can any human experience capture all of the elements necessary to guarantee an objective approach to the biblical text so as not to impose preconditioned conclusions of experience and culture on the text. Only as experience is validated by the teaching of Scripture, as in the case of black evangelicalism, can it be considered revelatory.

What must be done when addressing cultural concerns and experience through Scripture is to clearly understand the questions that the culture or experience is raising, take those questions, and place them parallel to a biblical question that was asked or raised in Scripture. Next, find the answer to that question from Scripture, and, finally, apply the answer to the question. Any other approach is subjective and does not align one's thought under the comprehensive rule of God. It forces one to make God and His revelation servants to man rather than having God as the final spokesperson. This asks experience to exegete Scripture rather than letting Scripture exegete experience.

The exegesis of culture and experience is indeed a valid enterprise, but only the exegesis of Scripture is an absolute enterprise. Culture and experience may raise the vital and necessary questions and may even illustrate divine answers, but they can never be the starting point for determining the meaning of Scripture. A partial approach to Scripture will never lead to full truth.

We, as African Americans, have been subjected for hundreds of years under the result of an incomplete hermeneutical approach to Scripture. We have been deeply impacted by such an errant methodology. Knowing this, we should be especially careful not to fall prey to doing the same. It can be safely argued that white Christianity did, and even still does, a partial interpretation of Scripture in its maintaining, or failing to seek to reverse, structural sins of dehumanizing separation, disparity, and subjugation brought about by past cultural sins of slavery and legalized racism whose generational effects remain in place at various levels.

James Cone, three decades after first publishing his thoughts on black theology, summarized a common concern still lingering among many:

> What deepens my anger today is the appalling silence of the white theologians on racism in the United States and the modern world. Whereas this silence has been partly broken in several secular disciplines, theology remains virtually mute. From Jonathan Edwards to Walter Rauschenbusch and Reinhold Niebuhr to the present, progressive white theologians, with few exceptions, write and teach as if they do not need to address the radical contradiction that racism creates for Christian theology.[1]

Many white theologians are, through a silence on the societal sins brought about by racism and classism, "wittingly or not, accomplices of and contribute to the maintenance of patriarchalism, racism, *apartheid*, and oppression in a variety of its psychological, social, economic, or cultural forms."[2] This may sound harsh, but if it were not a plausible reality, slavery's legacy of a sustaining of the great racial divide—the deepest stain on the soul of our historical American Christianity—would be addressed and amended with the same passion and zeal that other cultural sins and mandates are given in the white church, such as the just defense of the sanctity of life and the spread of the gospel overseas.

A recent example hit me hard when the obviously brutal and inhumane death of George Floyd at the knee of a white police officer went largely ignored by my white brothers who pastor large churches or lead large ministries. I recall commenting on the heinous public act on Twitter the day of his death. While we didn't know all of the surrounding circumstances at that time, I felt we knew enough, and could see enough, to say something against this very publicly inhumane action and ask God for His intervention of grace and mercy for the family, and those impacted by what they saw.

Yet as days, and even weeks, went by, I noticed that nearly none of my white brothers serving in spiritual positions of national influence and national platforms would say anything at all. In fact, they appeared to be so callous to the whole experience that seemed to traumatically shake an entire demographic of our nation, that they went on as usual, posting online about their new books or whatever meal they were currently consuming or social engagement they were having or speaking at. It seemed a bit . . . off.

Yet it was another stark reminder of the undercurrent of a great divide in interests, compassion, and a heart for the plight of those who still face the resultant ripples of a nation historically ransacked by racism. Silence is complicity. It is not enough to merely view racism as wrong, if a person is to live by the biblical standard of love. Rather, one must intentionally live as an opposing force to racism by actively seeking to change beliefs and behaviors that allow for its continual impact. And, at a minimum, demonstrate some level of empathy or compassion when an entire group of people experiences a very public display of collective pain.

While white theologians should carefully consider their biblical view on oneness, reconciliation, and, where applicable, biblical charity, those who adhere to the principles of black theology should also consider that through its experiential interpretational grid, it has likewise produced a fundamental flaw in that it is rooted in the black experience as that of a victim.[3] Both white theologians' silence and black theology's singular focus on racism promote separatism, thus limiting, through self-imposed means, the ability for the achievement of authentic biblical oneness.

What has been created and perpetuated through both is an enduring platform of separation that allows little opportunity for leadership development, evangelism and discipleship, racial reconciliation, personal responsibility, biblical justice, and cultural impact. Black evangelicalism seeks to place itself under the complete holistic authority of Scripture so as to provide a moral frame of reference under which all of life should align.

Ministry Development

Black evangelicalism seeks to define ministry within this context of holistic scriptural authority as any activity in which the needs of people are met by Christians in accordance with the Scripture. Events in themselves do not always help us address the societal crisis that we are facing, while ministry does. For example, the Bible never describes programs that are not tied to ministry. Unless a program serves the brothers and sisters in Christ or is an outreach to unbelievers in accordance with the commands of God, it is not biblical. For example, Acts 6 records a change in the ministry to widows in the early church. Because the Greek widows were being neglected in the daily giving of food, a complaint arose. When the apostles were told of the problem, they initiated a ministry in the church to work together to meet that social need.

Black evangelicalism recognizes the unique needs often present in urban or predominantly black congregations as reflective of the needs in the black culture. We are no longer a single-tier community; therefore, our churches need to reflect that reality both in the variety of ministries offered as well as their scope. Ministries must be multifaceted in order to deal with the great diversity of needs that are present. They must also relevantly address the unique needs of the next generation who are being governed, guided, and influenced by a whole new world of values and communication vehicles that have increasingly drawn them away from the Christian faith.

The Priority of Racial Reconciliation

Biblical racial reconciliation is a further emphasis of black evangelicalism, and kingdomology at large. While reconciliation has always been a desire of the black church, black evangelicals have taken an aggressive posture in order to implement this process with the broader white community.

Black evangelicals, to varying degrees, have historically lived in two worlds and possessed a double-consciousness—partaking of the black heritage, history, and experience while at the same time imbibing the biblical and theological influences coming from the white evangelical world. This has created, much like the black middle class, a hybrid.

Black evangelicals, therefore, are positioned in the distinct location of being able to promote oneness between the black and white church. Because black evangelicals have lived on both sides of the American ecclesiastical divide, we are uniquely placed to mediate the beginning of a new era of mutual benefit and integration among Christians who are culturally different, yet spiritually one.

The bridge of reconciliation has not been easy, on either side, and will continue to require humility on both sides due to the reality that bridges, by their very nature, are walked on from time to time. But the purpose of a bridge is also to take you somewhere that you would not have otherwise been able to go. The bridge of reconciliation takes us, in the body of Christ, to a place where the displaying of God's kingdom agenda is done in such a way that others may "see [our] good works, and glorify [our] Father who is in heaven" (Matt. 5:16).

If the chief end of man is to glorify God,[4] and as we have seen earlier through Jesus Christ's High Priestly Prayer that "complete unity" (reconciliation) brings glory to God, and that "good works" (biblical justice) also bring glory to God, then we can only reason that a unified effort of good works—reconciliation toward the aim of mutual service—is, and should be, a central objective to our daily Christian life.

Biblical racial reconciliation, as I have said throughout this book, is not an end in itself. It is a means to an end of glorifying God through good works done in a spirit of unity, with the goal of advancing His kingdom. Reconciliation can never be forced. It comes as the result of an authentic relationship built on mutual respect and understanding. Authenticity necessitates honesty. It also necessitates an acknowledgment of, repentance from, and subsequent forgiveness for the sin that initially caused the relational divide. Whether that repentance and forgiveness be private or public, it is critical that it be genuine and heartfelt.

America is an individualistic society. In many ways this is a positive quality; however, when it comes to addressing corporate sins, it can prove to be a hindrance. Christian whites have historically benefited from the systematic effects of racism, and yet those benefits are often so far removed from direct personal cause that a need for repentance in the area of racial reconciliation often goes unnoticed and unaddressed. But whether or not personal involvement in the sin has taken place, or to what degree it exists, is irrelevant to the biblical model given to us for corporate repentance when national sins have led to national effects. An awareness of this often comes to the surface in backroom discussions or, even at times, public ones. The example of Pastor Louis Giglio in his now infamous exchange with Lecrae, which left Lecrae virtually speechless in the moment, highlighted this.

In a video on racism and "white privilege" in America between Pastor Giglio, Lecrae, and Chick-fil-A chief executive Dan Cathy, Giglio referred to slavery in the context of it having been a "blessing." He said, "We understand the curse that was slavery, white people do. . . . And we say that was bad. But we miss the blessing of slavery, that it actually built up the framework for the world that white people live in."[5]

Pastor Giglio later went on to apologize for the statement, but the inference remained in the collective conscience of a culture already struggling with centuries of racism, oppression, and pain. To refer to slavery as a "blessing" through what it produced for businesses, systems, and structures of wealth in society for white people is a far cry from repenting for the evils committed both during and after slavery. What our nation needs from our spiritual leaders is a call to repentance and restoration through mutually shared good works especially for the poor and oppressed, not a dismissive nod at a past stain.

We see this biblical model in the books of Daniel and Nehemiah, where both prophets repented on behalf of their people. While doing so, both prophets included themselves personally in the prayer of repentance even though there is no indication that either prophet participated in the sin itself (Dan. 9:5, 7; Neh. 1:6–7). Thus, personal repentance on behalf of corporate sin that led to any degree of impact, benefit, or privilege for the corporate body ought to be offered in a like manner of sincere humility. When it is not, there runs the risk of cognitively diminishing as well as distancing oneself from the resultant effects of that sin in the lives of those who have been adversely impacted by it.

Likewise, forgiveness is often not acknowledged or granted on behalf of those who have been affected by the sting of historical abuses and institutional racism due to the corporate nature of the sin. Yet we as African Americans must apply the biblical principle of personal forgiveness modeled by Christ (Eph. 4:32), which will then release us from holding our white brothers and sisters hostage to any guilt or obligation toward us on a personal level. While we have every right to seek justice and resist ongoing manifestations of racism, we must also own our responsibility for personal development and progress through not seeking to illegitimately create, amplify, or take advantage of any presence of "white guilt."

Superficial racial relationships patterned on paternalism will dissolve before any lasting connection can be made. This is because "white guilt" produces a me-centered struggle for white redemption or white-heroics through liberalism rather than an others-centered focus on authentic connection, learning, empathy, and mutual respect. It keeps blacks stuck in identity politics relegated to inferiority, opportunism, or entitlement that can often perpetuate a mentality of victimhood. As Shelby Steele writes in his book *Shame*, "The benevolent paternalism of white guilt . . . had injured the self-esteem, if not the souls, of minorities in ways that the malevolent paternalism of white racism never had."[8]

Only through repentance and forgiveness done first and foremost on a personal level, which removes guilt and shame, will we be free to forge relationships that allow us to embrace dignity and diversity. We must be mindful that it takes time together in order to learn how to build trust, relate across cultural differences, and learn from each other. Unless our personal motivation is pure during the initial ups and downs of that time, we will become easily offended or wearied and fail to last in the ongoing effort that is required to learn how to embrace true oneness.

It is important to note that throughout the history of the church in America, there has always been a remnant of the white culture who, based on their capacity, intentionally sought out reconciliation, partnership, and a mutually respectful relationship with blacks in support of the black effort toward freedom and equality. This remnant has done so under their conviction of biblical justice and oneness, even when doing so meant great personal risk and sacrifice. These Christian whites have stood in the gap for their culture as a testimony of reconciliation and good works.

While that is true, a common challenge that has arisen in

attempts toward reconciliation among the broader white population as a whole, particularly in evangelicalism, is that the terms of oneness have often been set and established by the white community void of any substantive input on the front end by the black community. Reconciliation cannot be achieved by one group imposing its ideas, preferences, context, and programs on another. Nor can it be achieved by simply inviting the other group to participate in a program, an idea, or a ministry after the agenda and procedures have been established. This limits the contribution and intermingling of unique qualities needed in order to produce a stronger, more complete whole. It also reinforces the paternalistic practice of whites toward minorities. This was recently reflected in the Southern Baptist Convention when white seminary presidents rejected out of hand Critical Race Theory without first seriously including and interfacing with godly black leadership on what aspects of CRT, if any, might be valuable.[7] While they did meet with African American ministers roughly a month after the fact, a conversation ahead of time would have been much more appropriate.[8]

Both groups must be brought to the table on the front end of the discussion and planning so that there is full participation, recognition, appreciation, and use of the strengths of both groups. True reconciliation occurs through a merging of strengths toward the pursuit of a shared purpose under the lordship of Christ, not a begging to participate by a marginalized group to the in-group. Bryan Loritts addresses this rift in contemporary evangelicalism when he summarizes the thoughts of many black spiritual leaders seeking to be heard from a seat at the table:

> I'm tired of begging white evangelical academics to include people of color on their required reading lists. I'm tired of begging white homiletics professors to lengthen their references of good preachers to preachers of color. I'm tired of

urban hipster church planters, planting churches in gentrify-ing neighborhoods never once considering existing minority churches in those neighborhoods as ones to learn from and partner with.

I'm tired of recommending young minority leaders to serve on white church staffs, and watching them get used as tokens to show how "serious" the church is about diversity, only to see it end very badly. I'm tired of the silence of other minority leaders who, in their pursuit of climbing Mount Significance, are scared to speak the truth for fear of not being invited to some conference, missing out on a book deal, and not having their brand established or extended. I'm tired of the insensitive comments I'll get to articles like this from our white friends, not because it's pushback, but because they have grown up in all white churches that refuse to educate them on biblical, gospel issues like diversity and racial reconciliation.[9]

Both groups need to sit at the table but also both groups need to be heard. Both will also have to give up something, to yield in some areas, in order to fully implement the strengths of the other group; however, neither side should be asked to give up everything. Since true reconciliation is accomplished best through shared service, a plan should emerge designed to improve the lot of the poor, disen-franchised, and oppressed.

The Importance of Personal Responsibility

Black evangelicalism also emphasizes personal, family, church, and community responsibilities. Rights belong to God. Responsi-bilities belong to the people. These should not be lessened in light of systemic issues that make the implementation of wise life choices more difficult for many more blacks than whites in America. What the African American community needs to understand is that while racism is a problem and a challenge that must be ultimately addressed, it is not our chief adversary. While racism is real, it should no longer be viewed as determinative. It should not be seen as the primary impediment to our progress individually or as a people. How a person chooses to view something will have a large impact on his or her mindset, beliefs, and—ultimately—actions. If we would seriously take responsibility for the things we *do* control, then racism's negative impact can be greatly limited, and we would flourish more freely, personally and as a community.

This responsibility includes getting a good education and not dropping out of school; taking care of our families and not abandoning our marriages and children; getting regular health checkups, adopting overall healthy eating habits, and not abusing substances like alcohol, cigarettes, and drugs that are debilitating to our physical and mental well-being; as well as being honest and equitable in our dealings with those inside and outside of our own community.

Of particular concern is the growing and disproportionate number of abortions taking place in the black community, thus participating in what many feel is, and has been, a targeted genocide. The number-one killer among African Americans is not heart disease or cancer—it is abortion.[10] Since the legalization of *Roe v. Wade*, more than twenty million African Americans have lost their lives at our own hands due to abortion. To put this into context, in 1960 there were approximately eighteen million African Americans according to the census. Since 1973, abortion has killed more than the entire population in existence in 1960.[11] We must garner enough personal responsibility to analyze the data and ask ourselves why this is happening and why we, as a race, have been targeted in this way, while we are co-conspirators to our own genocide.

Other minority groups are increasing in size in America at a much quicker rate than the African American community, which is somewhat due to the increase in abortions among African American women.[12] African American women are five times more likely to have an abortion than white women.[13] According to the CDC, African American women (who account for approximately 7 percent of the national population) had the highest percentage of abortions performed between racial groups at close to 40 percent of all abortions. The abortion rate among African Americans was over three times higher than that of white Americans, and even higher than that of Hispanic women.[14]

Alveda King, the niece of the late Martin Luther King Jr., recently campaigned against Planned Parenthood when a light was shown on the founder, Margaret Sanger's, obvious eugenic aims as a member of the American Eugenics Society and a frequent speaker at events held by the Ku Klux Klan.[15] Alveda called the removal of a connection with Margaret Sanger at a New York abortion clinic, similar to the removal of confederate statues throughout the country, simply "window dressing." She went on to say, "Margaret Sanger sought what was an Aryan race, thinking that was more perfect . . ."[16]

This statement is reflected in Sanger's own writings, her own programs such as the "Negro Project" established in 1939,[17] and the legacy of targeting African American communities where nearly 70 percent of all clinics are within walking distance of urban, poor, minority-dominant neighborhoods.[18]

The church is complicit in our role in failing to own the responsibility for preserving our own lives. In fact, Margaret Sanger knew how powerful the African American church and our leaders were, so she specifically chose to use them to quiet any uprising against her attack on the Negro population. In a letter to Dr. C. J. Gamble dated December 10, 1939, she wrote, "The minister's work is also important, and also he should be trained by the Federation. . . . We do not want word to get out that we want to exterminate the Negro population and the minister is the man who can straighten out that idea if it ever occurs to their more rebellious leaders."[19]

The question on the table is, how can a community that has fought for the full expression of life as well as fighting against systems that would deprive us of that life join in on the destruction of life in our own community? We have turned a blind eye to what was clearly set up as our own participation in our own ethnic cleansing.

In addition, we must focus on where we can improve as a culture and strengthen our families and personal lives by promoting morality and the institution of marriage. We must stop excusing errant behavior in the name of racism. Even though racism was and is a major contributing factor to the decline of the black community structures, it is still our responsibility to take ownership for the things that are within our power to control. We cannot expect others to take us any more seriously than we are taking ourselves in addressing our needs. We must not illegitimately use racism as a convenient scapegoat for irresponsibility, mediocrity, or criminal and immoral behavior.

If a Super Bowl champion team complained when they took the field that there were eleven men on the other side of the ball trying to stop them, or if Michael Jordan had whined each time he took to the court that there was always someone in his face trying to block his shot, neither would have reached the goal they had set before them. While God is a God of liberation, God is also a God who divinely uses opposition as a tool that, when responded to correctly, develops perseverance, strength, determination, compassion, faith, and even, at times, greater and more personally satisfying opportunities than what would have been granted without it.

Jesus Christ does not guarantee freedom from racism, classism, sexism, or oppression while we still live in a sinful world. What He does promise is freedom from personal sin and strongholds coupled with the provision of the power to overcome. Although this freedom may not change the world, it will change each of us by giving us a divine perspective through which to deal with the problems that we face. What good is it to be at peace with your neighbor and not be at peace with God or yourself? What good is it to gain freedom from others and still be a slave to yourself?

Without a biblical view toward the principle and practice of overcoming adversity, a victim mentality takes root. This victim mentality bears the fruit of foreshadowing a wrong conclusion, thereby casting a self-fulfilling vision of limitation brought about in the context of having been, or being, at the mercy of someone else's intentions. Victimology exists far more than it should within black culture today and serves as a constant reminder of the obstacles blocking the movement toward forward progress. Unfortunately, it has become our own internally based form of oppression.

Black evangelicalism emphasizes the *truth* in the statement that it is in knowing the *truth* that one is set free. This truth includes the good, the bad, and the ugly. It includes principles on personal responsibility, sin, accountability, spiritual power, and authority, along with a need for pursuing a right relationship with God based on the foundation of His work in Christ and our identity with Him.

We cannot afford to be like the children of Israel who let the influence of more than four hundred years of servitude in Egypt keep them from moving forward to experience the promised land that God had for them (Num. 13–14).

The Prominence of Biblical Justice

Increasingly, concerted efforts are being made to address the ethical issues of our day; however, a lack of properly applied biblical justice is the underpinning for the continuation of societal and familial breakdowns as well as class and racial disparities. Biblical justice, when carried out correctly, naturally leads to the improvement of race, gender, and class divisions.

We read in this chapter that the Israelites sought God's help and assistance—what we could call His "blessings." In fact, it says, "Yet they seek Me day by day and delight to know My ways" (Isa. 58:2). Not only did the Israelites seek God, but they also fasted (v. 3) in a desire to experience the "nearness" of God (v. 2). Basically, they went to church, read their Bibles, prayed, sang, humbled themselves, and attended their small group studies. Yet, despite all of that, God did not respond to their pleas to bless them, nor did He respond to their requests for Him to execute "just decisions" (Isa. 58:2) on their behalf. Starting in verse 5, we read His reason why. It says,

> Is it a fast like this which I choose, a day for a man to humble himself? . . . Will you call this a fast, even an acceptable day to the LORD? Is this not the fast which I choose, to loosen the bonds of wickedness, to undo the bands of the yoke, and to let the oppressed go free and break every yoke? Is it not to divide your bread with the hungry and bring the homeless poor into the house; when you see the naked, to cover him; and not to hide yourself from your own flesh? (vv. 5–7)

Essentially, what God told the Israelites, in my Tony Evans translation, is that seeking Him, going to church, having regular prayer meetings, and the like was not enough. Because in spite of all of that, their relational actions revealed a contradictory reality, which showed that they were fasting as a means of argument while pursuing their own desire (Isa. 58:4).

The problem occurred in that their theology never affected their sociology. The thing they offered an "amen" to on Sunday never got carried out on Monday. They would come to church and sing about love, but return to the world and withhold that love. They would proclaim unity, charity, and equality in the house of God, but fail to practice that unity in the global body of Christ. Thus, the missing component of their ethical relational outworking within their theology nullified their religious activity.

The interesting thing about this passage is that what the Israelites sought from God ("just decisions") was the very thing that He says they withheld from others. Simply stated, the principle is: whatever you want God to do for you personally, you must be willing for Him to do through you to others. God is not looking for cul-de-sac Christians. He is looking for Christians who are willing to be a conduit of His blessing and justice to those in need (Luke 6:38).

It is not right to say, "Lord, help me," but then not help someone else whom you can. We cannot say, "Lord, deliver me," but refuse to be the deliverance for another person in need. That is contradictory Christianity. What we have often done in the area of biblical justice is relegate it to others while at the same time complaining to God that He is not responding to our needs. We have neglected to see that the two are often interlinked.

Also, while many of us do not directly carry out overtly unjust actions against others on a regular basis, the importance of biblical justice has become diminished in our minds. But the critical aspect to note concerning biblical justice is the biblical definition of sin. Because a sin is not only a wrong action that is done, but a sin is also a right action that remains undone (James 4:17). The question of biblical justice is not simply, Have I done anything wrong? The question is, Have I done what is right? It is good that you do not hate your brother or sister in need, but what are you doing to show that you love him or her by meeting a need? Isaiah 58 reminds us that the foundation for biblical justice exists in the principle that our horizontal relationships must accurately reflect our vertical beliefs about God, or we will limit God's response to our needs as well. Conversely, serving the oppressed frees God up to support our righteous causes.

James clearly tells us that "pure" religion is to "visit orphans and widows in their distress" (James 1:27). Orphans and widows represent the helpless and marginalized in society, those who cannot defend or empower themselves. This prescription isn't about what we do *against* the needy and the poor, it concerns what we do *for* them.

God says that He will do for us in response to what we do for others. Biblical justice is not a passive awareness of human needs, but rather an action taken to execute God's justice in the midst of an unjust society. Only when our biblical theology leads to a just and righteous sociology does God promise to make our lights shine, answer our prayers, and make us successful agents of reconciliation (Isa. 58:1–12; 2 Cor. 5:18–19). The distinctives of black evangelicalism is that its concern for biblical justice is intentionally married to personal evangelism and discipleship. Help on earth should always lead to the hope for heaven.

The Responsibility for Evangelism and Discipleship

While the black church has always been concerned about the salvation of souls and the spiritual development of its congregants, black evangelicals, utilizing many of the strategies and tools developed by white Christian organizations, began to put a major focus on black Christians being equipped to, in a formalized way, share their faith as part of their personal Christian responsibility and not just leave it up to the preacher on Sunday.

In addition, black church leaders were challenged to prioritize developing a formal discipleship focus and plan for their membership that went beyond Sunday school class. This emphasis included the development of Bible courses, theology classes, small group accountability and fellowships. Since the goal of discipleship is the replication of the character of Christ as a lifestyle based on the understanding and application of Scripture, black preachers were encouraged and challenged to develop a greater didactic approach to their preaching so that a greater focus would be put on biblical literacy. This, however, was to be done without losing the uniqueness of the black preacher's ability to connect truth to life through storytelling.

Black evangelicals placed a heavy emphasis on developing a more biblically trained clergy so as to meet the post–Civil Right's need for preachers who could effectively speak into the new contemporary world that black people were now entering with the increased diversity of thought, education, exposure, opportunity, and spiritual options available to them.

This increased emphasis on evangelism and discipleship, however, was never to dull the focus on the need to address the challenging realities of black life. Rather, black evangelicals incorporated social engagement as part of the discipleship responsibility of growing Christians. This engagement, however, was to be done with the goal of not only improving people's lives but also winning them to Christ and seeing them develop spiritually.

THE PRESENT STATE OF THE BLACK EVANGELICAL MOVEMENT

While none of us are completely removed from a connection to our own personal experience, black evangelicalism adheres to the conviction that we are not to allow our experiences to have an authoritative hold when it comes to interpreting and applying Scripture, whether that be a black experience, white experience, or any color. The Scripture assumes itself to possess a basis of authority and priority that transcends cultural distinctives and needs regardless of how tightly woven that experience is in the lives of the audience involved. When a theology based on experience rather than a biblical exposition of revelation is applied, interpretational and applicational methods of study are concomitantly transposed, leading to incomplete conclusions and diverting us from living out a kingdom-based model for life, especially in the areas of racial relationships and social justice.

The black experience is real, but not revelatory. It is important, but not automatically inspired. Recognizing this to be true during the social and theological revolution of the 1960s and 1970s placed theologians like me at the critical juncture of the emergence and development of black evangelicalism, in a position of being caught between two worlds. Holding tenaciously to a conservative hermeneutic of theology gave us, black evangelicals, a link to the white evangelical world. However, we also had to respond, both personally and on behalf of our calling given by God of faithfully and accurately shepherding those under our care, to the valid questions raised by the black revolution, black power, and black theology along with the inconsistencies taught by many of our white mentors.

As a result, black evangelicals serve in a long line of strategic links to help strengthen the ministry of the black church while simultaneously educating the white church to the far-reaching cultural impact of the gospel. The enslaved black church married the best of African religion and culture with the Christian faith to forge a unique imprint on the American religious scene. In the same way, black evangelicalism facilitated the fusion of the best of the black church with the best of the white church to hew out what could very well have been the strongest contemporary expression of biblical Christianity in America. The current divisions that plague us as Christians in our nation have sought to redefine many of the terms we have looked at in this chapter and in this book. And, often, rightfully so. Yet we still face a culture and a world in decline with a seemingly inept approach at addressing the real issues of the day. It is my belief that we will only experience the full expression of biblical Christianity in our nation, and in our world, if and when we are willing to come together underneath the overarching rule of God in every area of life—respectfully, as one.

While hugely important in shaping the history and even current structures of the conservative Christian black experience in our nation, the organized black evangelical movement has waned in its influence over the years. This applies both to the overall group as well as organizations such as the NBEA. For example, in the 1970s and early 1980s, the NBEA conferences and teachings were highly regarded. Yet following its peak in the early '80s, it began to decline as many of its younger members began to grow and develop our own ministries and focuses, which eventually proved to be larger than the NBEA itself. This specific organization was crucial during the embryonic days of evangelical integration and once stood alone in addressing the social issues at large, but these concepts then filtered into larger ministries, schools, and even cross-cultural institutions as the overall cultural climate matured on social issues.

In addition, personally, it was hard to stand with organizations such as the NBEA when they began to experience what many of us felt was a theological drift. That is why Ruben Conner, Eddie Lane, and I submitted our official resignation from the NBEA Board of Directors in 1980 due to what we saw as too much of a non-biblical framework influencing the conferences and dialogues.[20] Going too far to satisfy the black experience at the expense of biblical clarity had birthed what I and others believed to be an unclear gospel message that many of us could no longer align with. Thus, our commitment, and many others like us, to biblical inerrancy had placed us between two distinctly divided worlds once again. Had the concept of *kingdomology* existed at that time as a movement, I'm sure I—and many others—would have embraced it. But it didn't. It was still germinating in the seeds of the minds of those of us seeking to know God's heart for both the social and spiritual in the context of His overarching rule and role in our lives as His followers.

The author of Hebrews tells us that when God is ready to do something new, He creates a disturbance (12:25–29). The reason He creates the disturbance, according to Hebrews, is to shake earthbound and physical things up in order to reveal that which cannot be shaken. In other words, God shakes our physical, human reality in an effort to get us spiritually back on point. At the center of His purpose is the revealing of His unshakable kingdom.

I don't think anyone would disagree with me when I say that the black evangelical movement has been shaky over the recent years. In fact, I don't think anyone would disagree with me to suggest that evangelicalism, at large, has been shaken too. I would like to suggest that one reason for these disturbances is that evangelicalism (black and white) has gotten off-point. Evangelicalism has lost its way. We are being written off, dismissed, critiqued, and criticized—often with just cause. The very Word we proclaim has fallen into disrepute. Not because the Bible isn't true or we don't believe the Bible as white or black evangelicals, but because the presence that we ought to have due to the truth of the Bible has not manifested in the culture as our Creator designed it to be.

We have become the outcasts, and not just because we are being persecuted for our faith but rather because we are being persecuted for our foolishness. This problem of race should never have been allowed to seat itself in the church of Jesus Christ for generation after generation after generation. When Paul dealt with it in Peter and the others, he dealt with it both swiftly and soundly. What's more, Paul didn't confront Peter with sociology, an essay, or theory. He confronted him with the very truth of the nature of the gospel we all claim to love and cherish so much. Paul let Peter know the position on racial segregation and prejudice he had taken that day was intolerable and misaligned with the gospel (Gal. 2:11–20).

Far too many evangelicals have not understood that while the gospel is narrow in content, it is broad in scope. The unity of the church is a gospel issue, and it is a gospel issue saints need to know about. We cannot dismiss it by calling on the content of the gospel that gets us, or someone else, to heaven—while we skip the scope of the gospel, which ought to change how we relate to one another on earth.

So, to help the church out today, God is calling us out too. God is confronting us. He is shaking up the culture to reveal what's going on. Since the church has become content to continue to use illegitimate diagnostic methodologies for determining relationships, fellowship, and unity, He is messing up the culture enough so that we can no longer get away with skipping the issues we need to address. To our shame, evangelicalism has become bedfellows with political parties and partisanship, social movements, and class conflicts rather than maintaining our true identity.

We've got too many Bible-believing churches, Bible-believing Christians, Bible believing books, Bible-believing programs that all give God a lot of respect—on paper. We're just not getting anything done. We're not making much progress. We're not demonstrating a King who is ruling a kingdom. Because if we were, the culture wouldn't skip us or marginalize us. No, they would come to us for guidance and direction. They wouldn't ignore us. Unfortunately today, we have become too evangelical and not kingdom enough. The Bible is all about the glory of God through the advancement of His kingdom. It is about the rule of God to which we are to be subordinate. And since we sit under divine rule, we need to act like it.

We serve a God who is demonstrating to us through the tumultuous times in our land and in our world that He is the builder of the only unshakable kingdom. He rules over all. And until we align ourselves underneath His overarching command and obey His commandments, it doesn't matter what we call ourselves or how many programs we fund or streaming services we hold or what color we are. It is only when we intentionally live our lives underneath God's rule that we will advance His kingdom agenda together.

FROM EVANGELICALS TO KINGDOMOLOGISTS

The historical black church in America was the greatest demonstration of biblical Christianity in the nation. This is so because without much significant social, economic, religious, or cultural support, it not only hewed out a dynamic biblically based religion order, but also a comprehensive approach to the application of biblical truth to all of life. It lived out a kingdom perspective and worldview unlike its white counterpart.

Since the glory of God through the advancement of His kingdom is the overarching message of Scripture and His goal in history, I believe it is time for black evangelicals to lead the way in graduating from the identification of ourselves as evangelicals, in light of its growing negative political, nationalistic, and racially charged connotations, to another biblical identity as *kingdomologists*.

Kingdomoligists are Christians whose mission is to become kingdom disciples who function as kingdom servants that make a kingdom impact in order to advance God's kingdom agenda. Again, the kingdom agenda is the visible manifestation of the comprehensive rule of God over every area of life. This ID transcends the limitations that have become tethered to the term *evangelical* without losing its biblical roots.

Since Jesus came to proclaim the good news of the kingdom, as kingdomologists we still incorporate our evangelicalism under the transcendent banner of God's overarching goal reflected in Jesus' instruction to His followers to pray "thy Kingdom come, thy will be done on earth as it is in heaven."

The kingdom includes both the saving content of the gospel as well as its comprehensive scope. Since there is absolutely nothing that sits outside of God's rule, kingdomologists seek to demonstrate, model, and reflect its comprehensive nature as we live all of life under the lordship of Jesus Christ. It is the goal of kingdomologists to bring about transformation in the four spheres of the kingdom—namely, the individual, family, church, and community (i.e., government) through the clear presentation and application of His inerrant Word.

Just like the historical black church modeled the kingdom in the worst of times, black evangelically minded Christians today are uniquely positioned to lead the way in calling culture to return to the King and the primacy of His kingdom agenda. As black kingdomologists, we can model to the broader body of Christ the comprehensive understanding and application of a kingdom worldview while simultaneously making a clarion call for the unity of the church that is so deeply needed if we hope to see God reverse the course of the social and cultural decay our society is now experiencing. This call involves challenging the black church to return to our historically uncompromising biblical foundation so that black culture and the black experience are informed, clarified, and when necessary, corrected by the authority of Scripture. Conversely, black kingdomologists can challenge the white church to cease and desist from uncritically wrapping the Christian faith in the American flag, thus supporting a flawed and false Christian nationalism. Additionally, black kingdomologists need to remind the white evangelical church that biblical justice is to receive the same level of focus and attention that is given to personal righteousness. In this way black kingdomologists serve as emulsifiers bridging the historical divide between black and white Christians and church traditions.

Brief Overview of Racism and Its Impact on Society

I dive deep into the topic of racism, systemic racism, and its impact on society in my book *Oneness Embraced*, but want to include a brief overview here as it does shed light on the context of the black church in America. Studying the black church while ignoring the realities of both racism and systemic racism in the formation of the minds and hearts of her members and leadership would be naïve. Thus, this appendix is a helpful insight into many of the "whys" behind the "whats" going on in our culture and church today.

Many people define racism in many different ways. This is due to the tremendous variety in both the practical and emotive experiences that form the perspectives through which life is viewed. I define racism as *the conscious or unconscious belief in the superiority of one race over another race or ethnicities, which manifests itself in a variety of dismissive, oppressive, or exploitive ways.* Racism shows up in the use of power, influence, resources, or communication that is employed to discriminate against, marginalize, exploit, and/or subjugate people of another race or ethnicity. When unaddressed prejudice gets married to power there is going to be an unintended pregnancy that will give birth to the evil of racism.

I have heard the assertion, as I'm sure you have, that "systemic racism" no longer exists. I often hear that from people who out of their next breath say that they are not racist, and some might even add that they never owned slaves. These two statements are often so closely tied together that it appears to be a defensive personal posture that seeks to negate the existence of systemic racism, or its consequences, so as to absolve any personal feelings of attachment to it. Anglo author Ken Wytsma connects this defensiveness to a need for personal comfort. He writes, out of a response to being told not to use the term "white privilege" in a talk at a Christian university, that it seems "our desire for comfort leads us to defensiveness when we are confronted with questions of race." He continues with a good question, "But when did our comfort become the driving value?"[1]

And while I agree that our laws and legal systems on paper have largely been addressed and corrected over the years, I would assert that certain cultural repercussions remain. Just like a football team may win or lose on paper, but perform very differently in the actual game, paper laws intended to help don't always produce equitable outcomes. This is because the carrying out of those laws, as well as the residual effects of the earlier laws, applies to people, not paper. Whenever you insert humanity into the equation, you've inserted sin, and sin invariably messes things up.

In addition, the targeted rampant funding and promotion of unhealthy lifestyle norms that have annihilated the framework of the black family in many areas in our land, not just in urban centers (such as values-damaging movies, music, abortions, drugs), have sealed in much of the systemic limitations and resultant self-sabotaging behaviors that show up in the inordinately high prison rate among black males, the frequency of teenage pregnancy and

abortion, single-parent homes, and a lack of initiative in career training and the seeking of advancement.

Many people do not recognize this, but another insidious form of
racism was the illegitimate use of welfare, which targeted and encouraged the destabilization of the black family. Welfare entered the scene
just as legally based racism was beginning to be eradicated through
the Civil Rights Act and other reforms. And while many claimed that
welfare was implemented in order to help lift the plight of the poor, it
took aim at that which would have helped the poor to lift themselves:
personal responsibility, the promotion of two-parent homes, and self-
respect. Rather than seek to train, or in the Christian terminology
"disciple," individuals to make every use of opportunities for personal
growth, welfare (and other policies like it) undermined the upward
mobility of certain segments of our society.

Discipleship, by its nature, intends to deepen and expand its
impact by speaking to life's challenges through the establishment of
a stronger spiritual foundation as the starting point, as opposed to a
sociological foundation.

Sociology, in and of itself, does not make good biblical theology. Nor does sociology, in and of itself, offer a strong framework
for discipleship. In fact, many of the sociological systems that have
been enacted in an effort to help lift black Americans (e.g., war on
poverty, head start, affirmative-action, etc.) have actually—from a
statistical standpoint—only compounded the issues within the black
communities through the dismantling of core building blocks such as
the nuclear family, personal responsibility, and self-worth.

In essence, the anti-poverty initiatives (while arguably well-
intentioned by many) subsidized the destruction of the strength of
the black man by seeking to replace the virtues of work with welfare.
This then helped lead to the dissolution of the black family. The
number of black children born to two-parent households before these
policies were enacted was roughly 75 percent. But over five decades

later, that number is now representative of the over 70 percent of black children born to single-parent homes. It has flipped. As former president Obama said in his talk on fatherhood as a then senator at the Apostolic Church of God in Chicago,

> We know the statistics—that children who grow up without a father are five times more likely to live in poverty and commit crime; nine times more likely to drop out of schools and 20 times more likely to end up in prison. They are more likely to have behavioral problems, or run away from home or become teenage parents themselves. And the foundations of our community are weaker because of it.[2]

History has shown this trend of negative outcomes to be true, no matter the racial demographic, when policies that remove or undermine personal responsibility and value are applied to any racial demographic through any set of systems, legal or not.[3]

It is my belief that racism has embedded itself not only in many individual hearts throughout our history but also, to varying degrees, in many of the structures of our society. Whether those structures are political, economic, legal, or many others, they impact how entire groups of people think and live.

Systemic racism is said to exist whenever racism has become part of the policies, procedures, and mindset by which a particular entity or societal structure operates. And while law-based systemic racism may have been overturned or done away with through nationwide reforms, the lasting implications of many of these systems can still be felt by many. Rather than get stuck in semantics over whether or not officially sanctioned "systemic racism" exists in our nation through governmental laws or simply its resultant cyclical and cultural effects, as believers we ought to be open to examining real life struggles and how to solve them.

Systemic racism recognizes that the sin of racism is, or was, not only a personal issue but a corporate one as well. In fact, systemic racism even recognizes that while individuals themselves might not be racist, the structures and entities in which these individuals live or function can be established and still run on racist policies, practices, ideals, and intentions. I have heard many people argue against systemic racism through arguing that not all people of a certain race are racist. But that is not what systemic racism is. To acknowledge that systemic racism exists is not the same thing as declaring all white people to be racist. Systemic racism speaks to the structures, policies, and institutions of a society and not to the entirety of the individuals who inhabit it.

Thus, I define systemic racism as *the presence, or cyclical resultant effects, of racist practices and processes embedded in and shaping the social, political, economic, legal, educational, religious, infrastructural, and medical systems and policies of a society—initially established and perpetuated by the government. These then overlap and interconnect in such a way as to give an unjust advantage of resources, rights, mindsets, and privilege for a majority number of one race, while denying or limiting it to a majority number of other races or ethnicities.* Systemic racism's impact over the decades loomed large and still impacts a myriad of things such as employment, education, housing, incarceration, health care, family dynamics, wealth gaps, and much more. Any system or structure through which racist realities flow, be they known or unknown, contributes to an overall inequitable opportunity for personal advancement or personal wholeness. These same principles can apply to class divisions or caste systems and have existed in other nations divided by ethnic or racial constructs. It is not only a white/black matrix, but depends on the nation and the group in power.

We are all aware of the evil system of slavery, which was a legal system enacted to oppress black people based on the color of our skin. But what many people do not realize is that when slavery was dissolved, the ideologies within it merely got embedded into other structures in society. So, while the practice of slavery was outlawed, the principles that undergirded it remained present through other legalized systems from the Black Codes to Jim Crow. Thus, when people point to slavery as a contributing factor to present-day issues, they are pointing to slavery and the resultant practices and policies that flowed out of it up until now.

Systemic racism impacted me personally in a number of ways. One of which was when I tried to enter the media ministry in my mid-thirties. I was turned down by every station I sought to get on at first, except for one in Houston. Some would even go as far as to tell me that a black speaker would offend too many of their white listeners. While there was no "law" stating a black preacher couldn't air his sermons on white-owned radio stations, there was an embedded cultural system in place denying equal opportunity and equal access for upward mobility in ministry for black preachers.

Now, does that mean every radio station listener was racist and would have been offended at that time? No. Did I think every white person was racist at that time because I couldn't get on radio stations to broadcast my sermons? No again. That's because the existence of systemic racism, or its cyclical outworking, does not mean that every white person in America is racist either. But what it did mean back then is that the system of Christian radio in the early 1980s and before functioned, to some degree, with unwritten yet very clearly racist processes and standards.

I have plenty of other personal illustrations where I have faced systemic racism. One took place when I was asked to go speak to a group of Christian golfers at a golf club. Those who invited me wanted me to come and teach the Bible in order to make a spiritual impact on the men. I went, but after I got there I discovered that the people who had invited me had brought me to a place that I could not join. I was welcome as a preacher but not as a person.

Not too long ago, the church where I pastor purchased the golf course near our church. I proposed buying the 155 acres of prime acres in the southwest section of Oak Cliff not because I liked golf. I don't. In fact, I don't even play. I wanted us to purchase it in order to have a say in what happens in our community. We own several hundred acres of land in this area for that very purpose—to invest in the well-being and maintenance of our urban community.

The interesting history about the golf course was that black people could not play on it until the 1990s. This is because blacks were not allowed to be members. That was the rule when the golf course was first created in the 1950s.

When the golf course turned into a membership ownership course some years later, it was no longer a law that kept black people from joining. The law got removed because our culture was changing and that was no longer viewed as acceptable. But even though the unjust law got removed, the system was still plagued with racism. For example, before a person could become a member, an existing member had to recommend you. That shouldn't be much of a problem until you find out that after you are recommended, two-thirds of the membership have to also vote for you.

So, let's say a white man recommends a black man to join the golf club as a member. He's going up against a system that states that two-thirds of his peers have to agree, which is why no black man was voted in until 1994. Not because there was a law against it. There wasn't. But there was a system in place that operated on racist principles.

But taking this further—let's say as a white man you are part of the one-third that voted to have the black man admitted to join. Or you are the white man who proposed he join. Well, you still lost because of the two-thirds who were the majority in the system. You could come out and argue that you are not part of the two-thirds and are not like those people. You could also argue that you are not a racist, and you could be absolutely right. But the point is that the system you were a part of was racist. Acknowledging the existence of systemic racism is not the same as saying that all white people are racist. But denying its existence out of a spirit of defensiveness or an honest lack of personal involvement is insensitive to the plight of the many impacted by it either in the past or present.

While there are varying views of the degrees to which systemic racism is being reflected in the categories of our lives today, one thing is clear: wherever it (or its repercussions) exists, or whatever you choose to label it, there are real issues plaguing millions of Americans today. And much of this shows up in affecting primarily lower-class black Americans (but certainly other sub-groups and class-groups). Rather than spend all of our time arguing semantics or trying to pin blame (or deflect it), we as Christ followers ought to acknowledge the issues at hand and righteously address them.

A person merely needs to walk through the urban center of Baltimore, where I grew up, to witness the inadequate facilities in place to provide equal educational opportunities to Baltimore minorities as compared to the educational systems in the suburbs. And while admittedly there have been opportunities to address these issues through elected minority leadership, there has been an obvious failure to take advantage of those positions to bring about a greater good for the community at large. Historic systemic corruption can become so deeply embedded that it can show up even in those who you would think would want to change it.

As recently as 2020, graduation rates in the urban areas of Maryland were only 69.9 percent, while the average rate for the entire state is much higher at 86.7 percent.[4] Not only that, graduation requirements have been so grossly lowered in the urban schools that the Baltimore City Community College reported that 93 percent of all incoming students (70 percent of whom come from Baltimore's city schools) required remedial classes.[5] Lowering standards does not prepare an individual for success. In fact, it often sets them up for "induced" failure, which then contributes to a lowering of their own personal esteem through the concept of "mismatched" placement, which can then be handed down generationally, according to famed black economist Thomas Sowell.[6]

Systemic racism isn't a politically neutral issue either, as both sides often like to believe. Both sides of the aisle have contributed to its generational mess. In fact, much of it has been produced most recently through what people have labeled liberal "progressive" legislation and policies, beginning in the mid-1960s with the war on poverty. Any policy that seeks to strip individual responsibility, belief, confidence, and values from people, or dismantles the primacy of the nuclear family, does more harm than good.

In fact, looking at the statistics of racial income gaps prior to the war on poverty and other civil rights legislation and after it, it has remained the same, if not worsened in some areas.[7] Liberal policies, along with an errant view of the legitimate divinely created scope of civil government, fall short in producing the outcomes they claim they will. Rather, they produce an unhealthy and illegitimate dependency on government.

Shelby Steele describes this conundrum between liberal ideology and outcome as the "great internal contradiction of white liberalism: that its paternalism, its focus on whites rather than on blacks as the agents of change, allows white supremacy to slip in the back door and once again define the fundamental relationship between whites and blacks. . . . Whites are agents; blacks are agented."[8] Elsewhere in his book, Steele describes neither (liberal or conservative) side's true solutions in the context of his father's life. He was gainfully employed as a truck driver yet unable to join the Teamsters union, thus receiving less wages. He also had to hide his home ownership from his employer in fear of being fired for "getting above himself." Steele said his father thus lived in "an insecure nether land with no harbor among either capitalists or socialists."[9] In summary, "His society quite literally labored to defeat his ambition even as it left him entirely responsible for his life and family."[10]

Systemic racism, or its ensuing effects, often comes stacked over a lifetime, but it can also be viewed like dominos standing on a table. If you knock one domino over, the rest will likely fall. When children and youth are not given opportunities to excel in education (opportunities typically arisen out of a strong nuclear family, limited exposure to damaging influences, strong role models, healthy food and life balances, church, and an accurate view of personal potential), their opportunities for social and vocational successes diminish later in life as well. One thing leads to another. And this then is passed down generationally as poor life choices lead to generational consequences stacked on each other in what can appear to outsiders as communal self-sabotage. The net result is that hopelessness rules. Whenever hopelessness rules, chaos ensues.

Give a person hope and you have given them the structure within which to make healthy choices. What racism and systemic racism has done, by and large, is strip large segments of society of their hope, thus disempowering them toward their greatest kingdom expression of their dignity. But racism, however pervasive, should never be used as an excuse for not maximizing one's God-given potential or utilizing available opportunities. Again, even when being victimized, we must never succumb to the temptation of viewing ourselves as victims, but rather as victors who overcome.

Notes

Chapter 1: The Importance of Understanding History

1. Bob Jones III, quoted by Robert Sherrill, "Bob Jones University: New Curricula for Bigotry," *The Nation* (March 29, 1965), 326–33. The article was later reprinted in Robert Sherrill, *Gothic Politics in the Deep South: Stars of the New Confederacy* (New York: Ballantine Books, 1969), 248–49. For background, see also Bob Jones Sr., *Is Segregation Scriptural* (Greenville, SC: Bob Jones University Press, n.d.), a booklet transcribed from an April 17, 1960, radio address.

2. Philip Yancey, *Where the Light Fell* (New York: Convergent Books, 2021). See also Maina Mwaura, "One of America's Favorite Christian Authors Finally Tells His Own Story," Baptist News Global, November 15, 2021, https://baptistnews.com/article/one-of-americas-favorite-christian-authors-finally-tells-his-own-story/.

3. E. K. Bailey and Warren W. Wiersbe, *Preaching in Black and White: What We Can Learn from Each Other* (Grand Rapids, MI: Zondervan, 2003), 105.

4. Daniel Silliman, "Promise Keepers Tried to End Racism 25 Years Ago. It Almost Worked," *Christianity Today*, June 21, 2021, https://www.christianity-today.com/2021/july-august/promise-keepers-racial-reconciliation-reconsid-ered.html.

Chapter 2: The Myth of Inferiority

1. Jawanza Kunjufu, *Countering the Conspiracy to Destroy Black Boys*, vols. 1 and 2 (Chicago: African American Images, 1985).

2. William Banks, *The Black Church in the United States: Its Origin, Growth, Contributions, and Outlook* (Chicago: Moody, 1972), 9.

3. Hank Allen, "The Black Family: Its Unique Legacy, Current Challenges and Future Prospects," in *The Black Family: Past, Present and Future*, ed. Lee N. June (Grand Rapids, MI: Zondervan, 1991), 18.

4. See the "Curse of Ham," *Dictionary of Christianity in America* (Downers Grove, IL: InterVarsity, 1990), 333, for a summary of the argument and how it was used by the Christian church to justify slavery in America.

5. C. F. Keil and F. Delitzsch take this view in "The Pentateuch," *Commentary on the Old Testament*, vol. 1 (Grand Rapids, MI: Eerdmans, 1987), 178: "The Phoenicians, along with the Carthaginians and the Egyptians, who all belonged to the family of Canaan, were subjected by the Japhetic Persians, Macedonians, and Romans; and the remainder of the Hamitic tribes either shared the same fate, or still sigh, like the Negroes, for example, and other African tribes, beneath the yoke of the most crushing slavery."

6. In his note on the descendants of Noah's three sons in Genesis 9, Scofield remarked, "A prophetic declaration is made that from Ham will descend an inferior and servile posterity (Gen. 9:24–25 ix. 24, 25)." C. I. Scofield, *The Scofield Reference Bible* (New York: Oxford University Press, 1909), 16 n5. This note is repeated in the 1917 edition.

7. William W. Sweet, *The Story of Religion in America* (Grand Rapids, MI: Baker, 1973), 170, 285.

8. For a summary of how the slaves responded to this strategy, see Charles V. Hamilton, *The Black Preacher in America* (New York: William Morrow, 1972), 37–46.

9. Martin Luther King Jr., *All Labor Has Dignity*, ed. Michael K. Honey (Boston: Beacon Press, 2012), 194. These words were part of Dr. King's last speech on March 18, 1968, an address to Memphis sanitation workers.

10. Bill Duke, "As a Child I Tried to Drink Bleach after Being Teased for Being Dark," part 3, YouTube, May 12, 2019, www.youtube.com/watch?v=-uICZeiyUmE.

11. Ibid.

12. C. Eric Lincoln and Lawrence H. Mamiya, *The Black Church in the African American Experience* (Durham, NC: Duke University Press, 1990), xi.

13. Shelby Steele, *The Content of Our Character: A New Vision of Race in America* (New York: Harper Perennial, 1991), 17.

14. John M. Perkins, *One Blood: Parting Words to the Church on Race and Love* (Chicago: Moody, 2020), 85.

15. Charles Creitz, "Civil Rights Activist Bob Woodson Slams New York Times' 'Diabolical' 1619 Project on 'Life, Liberty & Levin,'" FoxNews.com, March 8, 2020, www.foxnews.com/media/civil-rights-leader-slams-diabolical-new-york-times-1619-project-white-supremacy-to-assume-all-african-americans-are-victims.

Chapter 3: *The Black Presence in the Bible*

1. See "The Search for Adam and Eve," *Newsweek*, January 11, 1988. A secular anthropologist and a scientist grapple with the data indicating Adam and Eve were African.

2. Walter McCray, *The Black Presence in the Bible: Discovering the Black and African Identity of Biblical Persons and Nations* (Chicago: Black Light Fellowship, 1990), 9.

3. Lerone Bennett, *Before the Mayflower: A History of Black America* (Chicago: Johnson Publishing, 1969), 5.

4. See my book coauthored with Dwight McKissic, *Beyond Roots II: If Anybody Asks You Who I Am* (Woodbury, NJ: Renaissance, 1994), for a comprehensive perspective on the role of black people in history.

5. McCray, *Black Presence in the Bible*, 31: "Black people need to understand all Black history, including that which is revealed in the Bible. If we are ignorant of our history and its heritage we will walk blindly into our future. And without keeping in our minds and hearts the spiritual and eternal dimensions of our history, our future forebodes a hopelessness which many of us would rather not face. From a Christian viewpoint it is important for Black people to understand their biblical history. Understanding the Black presence within the Bible nurtures among Black people an affection for the Scripture and the things of the Lord. Far too many of our people reject the Bible because they don't understand that it speaks responsibly about them and to their experience. God is concerned about Black people. Furthermore, enough information pertaining to Black people and their experience is written in His Word to convince the honest searcher for truth that God is indeed concerned for the well-being, salvation and liberation of Black peoples throughout the world."

6. Brown, Driver, and Briggs, *A Hebrew-English Lexicon of the Old Testament* (London: Oxford University Press, 1968), 871. The lexicon assigns the meaning to the root *KDR*, as "black-tinted."

7. See Brown, Driver, and Briggs, *Hebrew-English Lexicon*, 806, for the affinity between the names *Put* and *Putiel*.

8. Brown, Driver, and Briggs, *Hebrew-English Lexicon*, 20. See also Professor Charles Copher's discussion on "The Black Presence in the Old Testament," in *Stony the Road We Trod* (Minneapolis: Fortress Press, 1991), 151–52.

9. For other early usages of Niger, see Bauer, Arndt, Gingrich, and Danker, *A Greek-English Lexicon of the New Testament and Other Early Christian Literature* (Chicago: University of Chicago Press, 1979), 539.

10. J. Daniel Hays, "The Cushites: A Black Nation in the Bible," *Bibliotheca Sacra* 153:612 (October–December 1996): 398.

11. For an exhaustive scholarly treatment of the meaning, significance, purpose, and interpretation of the Table of Nations for understanding and validating the black presence in Scripture, see Walter McCray, *The Black Presence in the Bible and the Table of Nations: Genesis 10:1–32* (Chicago: Black Light Fellowship, 1990).

12. Egypt is identified in Scripture as the land of Ham (Pss. 78:51; 105:23, 26–27; 106:21–22), thus giving the ancient Egyptians a black ancestry.

13. Henry George Liddell and Robert Scott, *Greek-English Lexicon* (London: Oxford University Press, 1995), 37. *Aithiops* properly, burnt-face (i.e., Ethiopian, Negro).

14. Gerhard Kittel and Gerhard Friedrich, eds., G. W. Bromiley, trans., *Theological Dictionary of the New Testament*, vol. 2 (Grand Rapids, MI: Eerdmans, 1987), 766.

15. *The Original African Heritage Study Bible* (Nashville: The James Winston Publishing Company, 1993), 1831.

16. Keith Irvine, *The Rise of the Colored Races* (New York: W. W. Norton, 1970), 19.

17. Justo Gonzalez, *The Story of Christianity*, vol. 1 (San Francisco: Harper, 1984), 173.

18. Walter Elwell, ed., *Evangelical Dictionary of Theology* (Grand Rapids, MI: Baker, 1984), 95.

19. Ibid., 74.

Chapter 4: *The Black Church's Link with Africa*

1. Leo Frobenius, *The Voice of Africa*, vol. 1 (London: Hutchinson and Co., 1913), 2.

2. Edith Hamilton, *Mythology* (New York: Mentor, 1969), 32–33.

3. "Corinth," *The International Standard Bible Encyclopedia*, vol. 1 (Grand Rapids, MI: Eerdmans, 1979), 773.

4. Gordon Fee, *The First Epistle to the Corinthians* (Grand Rapids, MI: Eerdmans, 1987), 2.

5. Cornelius Olowola, "The Concept of Sacrifice in Yoruba Religion," Dallas Theological Seminary ThM Thesis, 1976, 3.

6. Timothy Bankole, *Missionary Shepherds and African Sheep* (Ibadan, Nigeria: Daystar Press, 1971), 6. Quoted in Olowola's thesis.

7. W. E. B. DuBois, *The Negro* (New York: Oxford University Press, 1970), 113–14.

8. E. Franklin Frazier, *The Negro Church in America* (New York: Schocken Books, 1963), 9–19.

9. E. Bolaji Idowu, *Olodumare God in Yoruba Belief* (London: Longmans, 1962), 7.

10. Ibid., 38–47.

11. Ibid., 61.

12. Ibid., 41.

13. Ibid., 66.

14. Ibid., 42–43.

15. See Olowola, "The Concept of Sacrifice in Yoruba Religion," 119.

Chapter 5: The Uniqueness of the Black Church

1. Henry H. Mitchell, *Black Belief* (New York: Harper and Row, 1979), 109.

2. See William Banks, *The Black Church in the United States* (Chicago: Moody, 1972), 17, for a summary of the influence of the Great Awakening on the slaves.

3. See John Lovell Jr., *Black Song: The Forge and the Flame* (New York: Mac-Millan, 1972), for a comprehensive understanding of the music of the slave community.

4. "Story" in black religious tradition refers to the progressive activity of God within the black community whereby He works in and through them, in keeping with His biblical movement in the deliverance of Israel and development of the church, to bring about their personal and collective salvation and liberation.

5. Thomas A. Dorsey, "This Man Jesus" (Chicago: Thomas A. Dorsey Music, 1949).

6. Harold A. Carter, *The Prayer Tradition of Black People* (Valley Forge, PA: Judson Press, 1976), 47.

7. Ibid., 80.

8. Ibid., 48.

9. E. Bolaji Idowu, *Olodumare God in Yoruba Belief* (London: Longmans, 1962), 131.

10. D. A. Hagner, "Sanhedrin," *Zondervan Pictorial Encyclopedia of the Bible*, vol. 4:271–72. Hagner explains this dual role of the Sanhedrin when he says, "The Sanhedrin certainly had complete control of the religious affairs of the nation as the Mishnah indicates. The high court was the supreme authority in the interpretation of the Mosaic Law, and when it mediated in questions disputed

in the lower courts, its verdict was final. Beyond this, the Sanhedrin also governed civil affairs and tried certain criminal cases under the authority of the Roman procurator. The Romans were quite content to let subject nations regulate internal affairs, but there were, of course, always limits. They, for example, would have reserved the right to intervene at will." Thus Hagner says, "The Sanhedrin had every right to prosecute Jesus for alleged crimes whether religious or civil."

11. F. F. Bruce explains why this beating was illegal. "Even if condemned a Roman citizen was exempt from flogging. By the Valerian and Porcian Laws (passed at various times between 509 and 195 B.C.) Roman citizens were exempted from all degrading forms of punishment (e.g., beating with rods, scourging, crucifixion)." *The Acts of the Apostles* (Grand Rapids, MI: Eerdmans, 1968), 322.

12. Charles C. Ryrie, "Perspective on Social Ethics," in *Bibliotheca Sacra* (Chicago: Moody, 1959), 316.

Chapter 6: The Role of the Black Preacher

1. Quoted by H. Beecher Hicks Jr. in *Images of the Black Preacher* (Valley Forge, PA: Judson Press, 1977), from Jackson W. Carroll, "Images of Ministry: Some Correlates and Consequences," paper delivered at Emory University, Atlanta, Georgia.

2. Henry H. Mitchell, *Black Preaching: The Recovery of a Powerful Art* (San Francisco: Harper and Row, 1979), 65.

3. Richard Allen (1760–1831) was founder of the African Methodist Episcopal Church (AME), the first fully independent black denomination in the United States (1816). This came about after he and his ministry companion, Absalom Jones, left the St. George Methodist Episcopal Church in Philadelphia in 1787 over being forced to a segregated galley in the church. He then established the Free African Society (FAS), which was a mutual-aid society that assisted fugitive slaves and new migrants to the city.

4. Charles V. Hamilton, *The Black Preacher in America* (New York: William Morrow, 1972), 102.

5. Ibid., 32–36. Three of the four cultural transformations are identified.

6. Each individual is responsible before God for what he says (Matt. 12:36) and does (Rev. 20:11–15, Matt. 16:27). This means that the fundamental and foundational form of human government is self-government under God. Men, therefore, are accountable to operate with a divinely informed conscience (Rom. 2:14–15). The three institutional governments (family, church, civil) are to operate in such a way that they represent and reinforce God's moral law within their prescribed roles, responsibilities, and limitations.

7. Henry H. Mitchell, "Black Preaching," in *The Black Christian Experience*, ed. Emmanuel L. McCall (Nashville: Broadman, 1972), 54–55. Mitchell summarizes why the Africans' storytelling background adapted them so well to the Bible when he writes: "Blacks took the Bible seriously, and for reasons easily traceable to their African roots. In their African roots, they had known huge quantities of memorized material. Even now, the history, which is still more sung than written, is known by anybody. In one of the festivals, if the performer makes one mistake, at least 200 people will say, 'Whoa, go back.' I mentioned this because even though many of these men were illiterate, they came out of a culture where people (I Fa priests) memorized thousands of proverbs. In the Yoruba religion, they have sixteen Odus. Each Odu has two hundred proverbs or stories, so that some of those Yoruba priests may know about as much verbatim as we have in the whole Bible. When you go to them for leadership, guidance, or divination, these men can call it right up. This explains to a large extent the way in which blacks adapted themselves to the Bible. The Bible was largely reflecting the kind of culture out of which they came."

8. Richard Soulen, "Black Worship and Hermeneutic," in *Christian Century* (February 11, 1970), 169–70.

9. Henry H. Mitchell, *Black Belief: Folk Beliefs of Blacks in America and West Africa* (New York: Harper and Row, 1975), 97.

10. Ibid.

Chapter 7: *The Black Church and Black Movements*

1. Walter Elwell, *The Evangelical Theological Dictionary* (Grand Rapids, MI: Baker, 1989), 379.

2. "History," National Association of Evangelicals, www.nae.net/about-nae/history.

3. Harold John Ockenga, Foreword to Harold Lindsell, *The Battle for the Bible* (Grand Rapids, MI: Zondervan Publishing, 1976): "Neo-evangelicalism was born in 1948 in connection with a convocation address which I gave in the Civic Auditorium in Pasadena. While reaffirming the theological view of Fundamentalism, this address repudiated its ecclesiology and its social theory. The ringing call for a repudiation of separatism and the summons to social involvement received a hearty response from many evangelicals. It differed from Fundamentalism in its determination to engage itself in the theological dialogue of the day. It had a new emphasis upon the application of the gospel to the sociological, political, and economic areas of life."

4. "History," National Association of Evangelicals, www.nae.net/about-nae/history.

5. For a summary of the relationship of music to the theology of the black church, see James H. Cone, *The Spirituals and the Blues* (Philadelphia: J. B. Lippincott Co., 1970); and Harold Carter, *The Prayer Tradition of Black People* (Valley Forge, PA: Judson Press, 1976).

6. Debate raged because of the propositions of the German scholar Rudolf Bultmann, who contested the validity of miracles in Scripture and thus found it necessary to demythologize the Bible.

7. Also known as modernism, this is the major shift in theological thinking that occurred in the late nineteenth century. It is an extremely explosive concept. The major thrust was to contemporize the archaisms of language and thought of the ancient world into forms and images that were more conducive to the modern world.

8. Henry Louis Gates Jr., *The Black Church: This Is Our Story, This Is Our Song* (New York: Penguin, 2021), 96.

9. Ibid., 95.

10. The Bible college movement began to call for a reemphasis on the fundamentals of the faith to counteract the growth of liberalism. Out of the Bible college movement came the Bible institute movement, which became an auxiliary means of educating blacks. Schools like Moody Bible Institute and Philadelphia College of the Bible developed night schools for blacks and others who worked full-time and could not attend during the day.

11. For example, my alma mater, Dallas Theological Seminary, would not admit blacks until about 1968. DTS, which had long been a bastion of conservative Christian education and a school for producing conservative writers, thinkers, and expositors, kept the doors shut to blacks because of the cultural climate of the day. This was true for most evangelical institutions.

12. E. Franklin Frazier, *The Negro Church in America*, and E. Eric Lincoln, *The Black Church Since Frazier*, in one volume (New York: Schochken Books, 1975), 140.

13. Anthea Butler, *White Evangelical Racism: The Politics of Morality in America* (Chapel Hill, NC: University of North Carolina Press, 2021), 53.

14. Tom Skinner, "The US Racial Crisis and World Evangelism," sermon transcript of Urbana Student Missions Conference, 1970, https://urbana.org/message/us-racial-crisis-and-world-evangelism.

15. Ibid.

16. Erin Burnett interview of Ed Litton, "Incoming SBC President Speaks on the Study of Critical Race Theory," OutFront, www.facebook.com/cnn/videos/incoming-sbc-president-speaks-on-the-study-of-critical-race-theory/190453866414865/.

17. Immanuel Kant was a German philosopher who endorsed the enterprise of human thinking apart from the Scriptures, the church, and the state.

18. For more detailed information, see chapter 31 in John Hope Franklin, *From Slavery to Freedom: A History of Negro Americans* (New York: Alfred A. Knopf, 1968); also see William Brink and Louis Harris, *The Negro Revolution in America* (New York: Simon and Schuster, 1964).

19. For more information on the term "white evangelicalism," see Raymond Chung, "An Open Letter to John Piper on White Evangelicalism and Multi-Ethnic Relations," October 20, 2017, churchleaders.com.

20. Eric Mason, *Woke Church: An Urgent Call for Christians in America to Confront Racism and Injustice* (Chicago: Moody, 2018), 30.

21. Timothy I. Cho, "Interview: Eric Mason Talks Redeeming 'Wokeness' and Abandoning 'Evangelicalism,'" *Faithfully Magazine*, 2019, https://faithfully magazine.com/eric-mason-wokeness-evangelicalism.

22. "I've Been to the Mountaintop," speech by Martin Luther King Jr., April 3, 1968, Mason Temple, Church of God in Christ Headquarters, Memphis, Tennessee.

23. James H. Cone, *God of the Oppressed* (New York: Seabury Press, 1975), 3.

24. James H. Cone, "The Gospel and the Liberation of the Poor," *Christian Century*, February 18, 1981, 162.

25. James H. Cone, *Black Theology and Black Power* (New York: Seabury Press, 1969), 121.

26. Frazier, *Negro Church in America*, and Lincoln, *Black Church Since Frazier*, 192.

27. Benjamin Watson, *Under Our Skin: Getting Real About Race and Getting Free From the Fears and Frustrations That Divide Us* (Wheaton, IL: Tyndale Momentum, 2016), 91.

28. Most proponents trace its origins to the killing of Trayvon Martin, and its rise in prominence to the death of Michael Brown.

29. Sony Salzman, "From the Start, Black Lives Matter Has Been about LGBTQ Lives," ABCNews.com, June 21, 2020, abcnews.go.com/US/start-black-lives-matter-lgbtq-lives/story?id=71320450.

30. "'We Are Trained Marxists'—Patrisse Cullors, Co-Founder, #BlackLivesMatter," YouTube, June 19, 2020, www.youtube.com/watch?v=HgEUbSzOTZ8.

31. "What Is Critical Race Theory?," UCLA School of Public Affairs, https://spacrs.wordpress.com/what-is-critical-race-theory/: "CRT recognizes that racism is engrained in the fabric and system of the American society. . . . Legal discourse says that the law is neutral and colorblind, however, CRT challenges

this legal 'truth' by examining liberalism and meritocracy as a vehicle for self-interest, power, and privilege."

32. Quoted in Susan Ellingwood, "What Is Critical Race Theory, and Why Is Everyone Talking about It?," *Columbia News*, July 1, 2021, https://news.columbia.edu/news/what-critical-race-theory-and-why-everyone-talking-about-it-0. See also the discussion by Ibram X. Kendi, "There Is No Debate over Critical Race Theory," *The Atlantic*, July 9, 2021, www.theatlantic.com/ideas/archive/2021/07/opponents-critical-race-theory-are-arguing-themselves/619391/.

33. Other founders are typically considered to include Richard Delgado, Charles Lawrence, Mari Matsuda, Patricia Williams, and Kimberly Williams.

34. Derrick A. Bell Jr., "Who's Afraid of Critical Race Theory?," *University of Illinois Law Review* (1995), 893–910.

35. Angela P. Harris, "Foreword: The Jurisprudence of Reconstruction," *California Law Review* 82.4 (July 1994), 743.

36. Ibid., 743.

37. Bell, "Who's Afraid of Critical Race Theory?," 900.

38. Much of the opposition to CRT comes through the argument that Critical Legal Studies (CLS) was formed out of Critical Theory (CT), unfortunately without the concomitant research and dialogue to discuss what, if any, of CRT relates to CT itself. The concept of Critical Theory, also known as the "Frankfurt School," was first published in 1937 as "Traditional and Critical Theory" by Max Horkheimer at Columbia University in NYC.

39. Ibram X. Kendi, *Stamped from the Beginning: The Definitive History of Racist Ideas in America* (New York: Bold Type Books, 2017), 443. Some debate exists as to the exact official date of inception.

40. Ibid., 444.

41. Bell, "Who's Afraid of Critical Race Theory?," 899.

42. Derrick A. Bell Jr., "*Brown v. Board of Education* and the Interest-Convergence Dilemma," *Harvard Law Review* 93.3 (1980), 523.

43. See "The 90-Year-Old Financial Policy That Harms Our Health," NYC.gov, https://a816-dohbesp.nyc.gov/IndicatorPublic/Closerlook/redlining/index.html.

44. Voddie T. Baucham Jr., *Fault Lines: The Social Justice Movement and Evangelicalism's Looming Catastrophe* (Washington, DC: Salem Books, 2021), 164.

Chapter 8: The Rise of Black Evangelicalism and Kingdomology

1. James H. Cone, *Risks of Faith: The Emergence of Black Theology of Liberation, 1968–1998* (Boston: Beacon Press, 1999), 130.

2. Daniel Patte and Gary Phillips, "A Fundamental Condition for Ethical Accountability in the Teaching of the Bible by White Male Exegetes: Recovering and Claiming the Specificity of Our Perspective," *Scriptura* 9 (1991): 8.

3. Anthony B. Bradley, *Liberating Black Theology: The Bible and the Black Experience in America* (Wheaton, IL: Crossway, 2010), Introduction.

4. Westminster Shorter Catechism, answer to question 1.

5. Sarah Pulliam Bailey, "Atlanta Megachurch Pastor Louie Giglio Sets off Firestorm by Calling Slavery a 'Blessing' to Whites," *Washington Post*, June 16, 2020, www.washingtonpost.com/religion/2020/06/16/atlanta-megachurch-pastor-louie-giglio-sets-off-firestorm-after-calling-slavery-white-blessing (a video of the event is embedded in the article).

6. Shelby Steele, *Shame: How America's Past Sins Have Polarized Our Country* (New York: Basic Books, 2015), 2.

7. "Prominent Black Pastor Pondering Exit," ABCNews.com, abcnews.go.com/politics/wirestory/prominent-black-pastor-pondering-exit-southern-baptists-75456007.

8. "Seminary Presidents Meet with Black Pastors But Don't Change Position on Critical Race Theory," BaptistNews.com, baptistnews.com/article/sbc-seminary-presidents-meet-with-black-pastors-but-dont-change-position-on-critical-race-theory/.

9. Bryan Loritts, "More on Leaving White Evangelicalism: A Response from Bryan Loritts," *Christianity Today*, October 20, 2017, www.christianitytoday.com/edstetzer/2017/october/response-to-ray-changs-open-letter-to-john-piper.html.

10. Charlene Aaron, "The Number One Killer of All African Americans," CBN.com, July 8, 2019, www1.cbn.com/cbnnews/us/2019/june/the-number-1-killer-of-all-African-Americans-black-denomination-battles-the-racism-of-abortion.

11. Catherine Davis and Bradley Mattes, "Since *Roe* Abortion Has Killed More Black Babies Than the Entire Black Population of the US," *Washington Examiner*, www.washingtonexaminer.com/opinion/op-eds/since-roe-abortion-has-killed-more-black-babies-than-the-entire-black-population-of-the-u-s-in-1960.

12. "Resident Population of the United States by Race from 2000 to 2020," www.statista.com/statistics/183489/population-of-the-us-by-ethnicity-since-2000/.

13. Zoe Dutton, "Abortion's Racial Gap," *The Atlantic*, September 22, 2014, www.theatlantic.com/health/archive/2014/09/abortions-racial-gap/380251.

14. Katherin Kortsmit et al., "Abortion Surveillance—United States, 2018," Centers for Disease Control and Prevention, November 27, 2020, www.cdc .gov/mmwr/volumes/69/ss/ss6907a1.htm.

15. Mary Anne Dion, "Hitler, the Ku Klux Klan, and Margaret Sanger," *Courier Herald*, April 10, 2019, www.courierherald.com/letters/hitler-the-ku-klux-klan-and-margaret-sanger.

16. "Window Dressing: Alveda King Says NY Planned Parenthood Removing Aryan Racist Sanger from Clinic Not Enough," CBSNews.com, https://www1.cbn.com/cbnnews/us/2020/july/window-dressing-alveda-king-says-ny-planned-parenthood-removing-aryan-racist-sanger-from-clinic-not-enough.

17. Tanya L. Green, "The Negro Project: Margaret Sanger's Eugenic Plan for Black America," http://www.blackgenocide.org/negro.html.

18. "Is Planned Parenthood Targeting Certain Neighborhoods?," FoxNews.com, August 14, 2015, www.foxnews.com/transcript/is-planned-parenthood-targeting-certain-neighborhoods.

19. Margaret Sanger to C. J. Gamble, December 10, 1939, Margaret Sanger Papers, Smith College Library Archive, https://libex.smith.edu/omeka/files/original/d6358bc3053c93183295bf2df1c0c931.pdf.

20. Jimmy Lockyear, "Theology Culture Rift Surfaces Among Evangelical Blacks," *Christianity Today*, May 23, 1980, www.christianitytoday.com/ct/1980/may-23/theology-culture-rift-surfaces-among-evangelical-blacks.html.

Appendix: Brief Overview of Racism and Its Impact on Society

1. Ken Wytsma, *The Myth of Equality: Uncovering the Roots of Injustice and Privilege* (Downers Grove, IL: InterVarsity Press, 2019), 23.

2. "Text of Obama's Fatherhood Speech," Politico, June 15, 2008, https://www .politico.com/story/2008/06/text-of-obamas-fatherhood-speech-011094.

3. Thomas Sowell, "Affirmative Action: A Worldwide Disaster," *Commentary*, December 1989, https://www.commentarymagazine.com/articles/thomas-sowell-2/affirmative-action-a-worldwide-disaster/.

4. Chris Papst, "Baltimore City Schools Graduation Rate Drops to Six-Year Low," The Maryland Public Policy Institute, March 31, 2021, https://www.mdpolicy.org/research/detail/baltimore-city-schools-graduation-rate-drops-to-six-year-low.

5. Ibid.

6. Thomas Sowell, *Intellectuals and Race* (New York: Basic Books, 2013), 66–67. "A study at M.I.T, for example, showed that the average black student there had math SAT scores in the top 10 percent nationwide—and in the bottom

10 percent at M.I.T. Nearly one-fourth of these extraordinarily high-ranking black students failed to graduate from M.I.T. . . . In short, ignoring test scores and other academic qualifications when admitting minority students turns minority students with all the qualifications for success into artificially induced failures, by mismatching them with the institutions that admit them under lower standards."

7. Heather Long, "The Black/White Economic Divide Remains As Wide As in 1968," *Washington Post*, June 4, 2020, https://www.washingtonpost.com/business/2020/06/04/economic-divide-black-households/.

8. Shelby Steele, *White Guilt: How Blacks and Whites Together Destroyed the Promise of the Civil Rights Era* (New York: Harper Perennial, 2007), 147–48.

9. Ibid., 148.

10. Ibid., 149.

Subject Index

JOHN PERKINS SPEAKS WITH GODLY WISDOM TO HELP US UNDERSTAND ISSUES OF RACE AND JUSTICE.

MOODY Publishers®

From the Word to Life®

Civil rights hero Dr. John Perkins speaks with godly wisdom, grace, and many years of experience to help us understand race in America today. In *One Blood*, he speaks honestly to the church about—in his own words—"the things I've discovered to be crucial about reconciliation, discipleship, and justice ... the principles I believe to be vital to a complete ministry of reconciliation." In *He Calls Me Friend*, Perkins applies one simple truth about how to change the world: "Be friends. First with God. Then with others—every kind of other you can think of." And in *Count It All Joy*, Perkins helps you see your endurance in suffering as a virtue that makes you more like Christ and produces joy in those who trust Him.

978-0-8024-2397-9 | 978-0-8024-1936-1 | 978-0-8024-2175-3 | available as eBooks

"Between the Christianity of this land, and the Christianity of Christ, I recognize the widest possible difference."—Frederick Douglass, 1845